The Road to NYPD Retirement

A comprehensive retirement
planning resource for
active and retired NYPD members

Peter Thomann, EA, CFP®

ISBN: 0615731252

ISBN-13: 9780615731254

Library of Congress Control Number: 2012954457

CreateSpace Independent Publishing Platform

North Charleston, South Carolina

Thomann Tax & Asset Management Inc

Staten Island, NY

CONTENTS

INTRODUCTION

The purpose of this book is to provide the retiring and retired New York City Police Department (NYPD) member with a basic knowledge of retirement planning in order to make well-informed financial decisions. Retiring from the NYPD today is very different than thirty years ago. The modern day NYPD retiring member is faced with many decisions that have to be made, and often, these decisions are irrevocable. These decisions are related to when to retire, election of final distribution, New York City Deferred Compensation Plan distributions, rollovers, pension options, tax issues, union annuity plan distributions, etc. This book is not meant to provide all of the answers to these difficult decisions, but hopefully, the book will provide the reader with a solid understanding of the tax and retirement planning issues.

Note: Chapter 1, "The NYPD Pension," has two main sections. The first section reviews Tier II benefits and the second reviews Tier III benefits. Tier II members have an NYPD appointment date from July 1, 1973 through June 30, 2009. Tier III members have an appointment date from July 1, 2009 through March 31, 2012. Tier III–revised members have an appointment date from April 1, 2012 to the present.

Disclaimer: The information and examples provided in this book are illustrative and may or may not apply to the reader's particular situation. The material presented should not be construed as financial and/or tax advice. Reasonable efforts have been made to ensure the accuracy of the material.

1

THE NYPD PENSION

The idea of retiring from the NYPD after twenty years of service is very appealing. Yes, a few members may have been disciplined savers throughout their careers and have no family financial obligations and are able to ride off into the sunset and be fully retired. For the most part, NYPD members who retire after twenty years are moving on to a second career or to a less stressful job. As NYPD members get closer to their twentieth anniversary, they begin to analyze the advantages and disadvantages of retiring from the NYPD. For some, the decision is very simple and requires little analysis; the NYPD member retires at the twentieth anniversary and never looks back. For others, the decision is not that simple as a result of the current economy and the difficulty in obtaining a well-paying job, significant family obligations, debt, etc. The purpose of this chapter is to provide the pre-NYPD retiree with a better understanding of how the police pension is calculated at the twentieth year of service and also beyond twenty years of service. When it comes to trying to decide whether to retire from the NYPD; knowledge is critical. Pre-retirees should learn as much as possible in order to make a more informed and educated retirement decision.

Defined Benefit

The NYPD pension is considered a defined benefit pension and is funded by both the NYPD employee and by New York City (NYC). A significant advantage of the defined benefit plan for NYC Police Pension Fund members is that the investment risk is the responsibility of NYC. In other words, NYC and the NYC Police Pension Board have the task of investing the pension assets to ensure that a benefit will be available for pensioners. NYC Police Pension Fund members do not have to make any investment decisions; it is all done for them.

This defined benefit will be a critical component of a retiree's overall retirement funding mechanism. Ideally, NYPD retirees will have four sources of funds for retirement: defined benefit (pension), Social Security, retirement accounts (401k, 457b, IRA, etc.), and personal savings. With proper planning and disciplined saving, many NYPD retirees will be able to live comfortably in their retirement years.

Tier II

Required Amount

When an individual is hired by the NYPD and becomes a participating member of the NYC Police Pension Fund, that individual is assigned a specific contribution rate. The contribution rate, which varies by age of appointment, is a percentage of pensionable earnings that is required to be contributed to the NYC Police Pension Fund. These contributions are "required" for the first twenty years of service. Even though the contributions are required, members can elect to opt out of contributing and receive a reduced pension benefit. The required contributions made by the member over a twenty-year career and the interest earned on the contributions determine the required amount. The required amount is different for each NYC Police Pension Fund member because of different contribution rates, salary history, overtime, promotions, etc.

The increased-take-home-pay (ITHP) provision is associated with the required amount. Simply stated, the ITHP provision is the portion of the member's contribution rate that NYC pays. For example, an NYPD member is hired at age twenty-two and is assigned a contribution rate of 7.65%. Under the current ITHP rules, NYC will contribute 5% of the 7.65%. As a result, the member's contribution rate is reduced to 2.65%, which results in an increase of take-home pay. For the member to receive an unreduced pension benefit, this member would be required to contribute 2.65% of pensionable earnings for a twenty-year period.

Final Average Salary

The final average salary (FAS) is the starting point in determining the pension of a retiring NYC Police Pension Fund member. FAS consist of pensionable earnings: salary, night-shift differential, holiday pay, overtime, and longevity. It should be noted that the longevity at twenty years of service is pensionable at the completion of twenty-five years of service. Members retiring at twenty years of service and less than twenty-five years of service calculate pensionable longevity at the five- and ten-year levels.

Definitions of FAS vary, depending on date of appointment. For members who have an appointment date prior to July 1, 2000, there are three different methods available to calculate FAS:

- Final twelve months
- Final thirty-six months
- Three consecutive calendar years

Note: Members appointed July 1, 2000, through June 30 2009 can only use the final twelve months as FAS.

The FAS may be limited if pensionable earnings exceed the prior year or years by 20%. Table #1 is an example of the final twelve months FAS accounting for the "20% rule."

Table #1			
Year	Pensionable Earnings	Earnings Limit	Pensionable Earnings for FAS
20XX	$105,000	N/A	N/A
20XX	$128,000	$126,000	$126,000

The final twelve months immediately precedes the retirement date and does not have to be a calendar year.

Table #2 is an example in which three consecutive calendar years are used to calculate the FAS. In order to correctly calculate the three consecutive calendar years, the member needs to account for the two previous calendar years.

Table #2			
Year	Pensionable Earnings	Earnings Limit	Pensionable Earnings for FAS
20XX	$92,000	N/A	N/A
20XX	$90,000	N/A	N/A
20XX	$111,000	$109,200	$109,200
20XX	$115,000	$120,600	$115,000
20XX	$110,000	$135,600	$110,000
Three Year Average: $111,400			

Basic Twenty-Year NYPD Pension Calculation

Calculating a twenty-year-service retirement NYPD pension benefit is fairly simple, and much of the calculation is based on the member's Annuity Savings Fund (ASF) balance as compared to the member's required amount. The ASF consists of a member's contributions and the interest earned on the contributions. In order for a member to receive 50% of FAS, their ASF must equal their required amount.

For example:

- Number of years of service = 20
- FAS = $100,000
- Member's required amount = $95,000
- Member's ASF balance = $95,000
- Annual pension benefit = $50,000
  (2.5% × FAS × years of service)

Note: some members may also receive a benefit for prior non-uniform service.

If a member has less than the required amount in their ASF account, a shortage exists and the pension will be less than 50% of the FAS. If a member has more than the required amount in their ASF account, an overage or excess exists and the pension will be more than 50% of the FAS.

Shortages and Excesses

As described above, a shortage occurs when a member's ASF balance is less than the required amount. The following are possible causes of a shortage:

- Pension loan(s)
- Service transfers and buybacks
- Stopping pension contributions
- Contract settlement (back pay)

The following example shows the effect of a shortage when calculating the pension benefit:

- Twenty-year service retirement
- Member is forty-five years old at retirement
- Required amount = $90,000
- Member's ASF balance = $60,000
- Shortage = $30,000
- Member's FAS = $100,000

Calculation:

- 50% of FAS = $50,000
- Annuity value of shortage = $2,453
- Annual pension benefit = $47,547

Is it possible to make up a shortage? Yes, there are three different methods available that increase a member's ASF account and, therefore, reduce or eliminate the shortage.

- Lump sum contribution
- Waive ITHP
- 50% additional

The lump sum contribution can be used if the member has funds available to make a lump sum payment to the Police Pension Fund. If a member elects to waive the ITHP, an additional 5% of biweekly earnings are contributed to the member's ASF account. Please note that electing to waive the ITHP results in a reduction of the member's take-home pay. A benefit of the ITHP waiver is that the contributions are based on pre-tax monies, which reduce a member's overall current tax liability. The final method, 50% additional, is based on the member's contribution rate and funds the ASF account with after-tax monies. The following is an example of a thirty year old Police Pension Fund member contributing the ITHP waiver and the 50% additional:

- Age when hired = 25
- Contribution rate = 7.15%
- Current annual gross earnings = $95,000

Table #3			
Type	Rate %	Yearly $ Amount Contributed	Pre or Post Tax
Member rate	2.15%	$2,043	Pre-tax
ITHP waiver	5.00%	$4,750	Pre-tax
50% additional	3.575%	$3,396	Post-tax
Total	10.725	$10,189	

Reviewing Table #3, the member contributed $8,146 more than was required and reduced current taxable earnings from $95,000 to $88,207. Deciding whether to elect the ITHP waiver and/or the 50% additional is a personal choice and often depends on what the member can afford.

An excess in a member's ASF account is a result of the member contributing more than the required amount through the ITHP waiver and/or the 50% additional. At retirement, the excess can be withdrawn, rolled over, or left with the Police Pension Fund for an increased defined benefit. Many Police Pension Fund members are unaware of their ASF account balances and may be doing themselves a disservice by not taking advantage of an opportunity to earn a substantial rate of return on their money. Members who have an excess ASF balance understand the power of compounding interest when electing the ITHP waiver and the 50% additional. Graph #1 below displays the power of compounding interest along with ongoing ITHP waiver and 50% additional contributions compared with contributing only the required amount:

- Contribution rate = 7.15%
- ITHP waiver = Yes
- 50% additional = Yes

- Estimated annual salary from 15 to19 years = $110,000
- ASF balance at end of fourteen years of service = $90,000

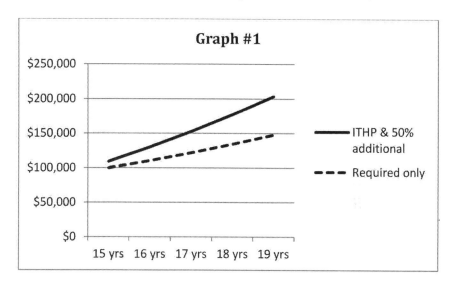

A review of Graph #1 indicates that the member who contributed both the ITHP waiver and the 50% additional had an ending balance of $203,302. The member who contributed only the required amount had an ending balance of $147,721.

Let's see what happens if we continue the same process for another 5 years:

- Contribution rate = 7.15%
- ITHP waiver = Yes
- 50% additional = Yes
- Estimated annual salary from 20 to 24 years = $120,000
- ASF balance for member contributing ITHP waiver and 50% additional at end of nineteen years of service = $203,302
- ASF balance for member electing to contribute the required amount only at end of nineteen years of service = $147,721

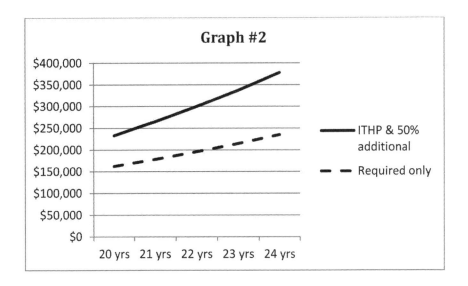

A review of Graph #2 indicates that the member who contributed both the ITHP waiver and the 50% additional had an ending balance of $378,036. The member who contributed only the required amount had an ending balance of $234,786.

Beyond 20 Years NYPD Pension Calculations

NYPD members benefit significantly by remaining on the job after twenty years of service. The basic pension formula for a member with more than twenty years of service is as follows:

- 50% of FAS
- Plus 1/60 of earnings after the twentieth anniversary
- Plus the annuity value of NYC ITHP contributions after twentieth anniversary
- Plus the annuity value of the excess over the required amount *or* less the annuity value of a shortage

Note: some members may also receive a benefit for prior non-uniform service.

The following is an example of a Police Pension Fund member who retired after twenty-two years of service and had an excess in the ASF account.

- Twenty-two-year service retirement
- Member is forty-seven years old at retirement
- Required amount = $90,000
- Member's ASF balance = $160,000
- Excess = $70,000
- Member's FAS = $110,000
- Earnings from twenty to twenty-two years = $220,000

Calculation:
- 50% of FAS = $55,000
- Value of 1/60 = $3,667
- ($220,000/60)
- Estimated value of NYC ITHP benefit = $1,002
- Value of excess = $5,844
- Annual pension benefit = $65,513

The following is an example of a Police Pension Fund member who retired after thirty years of service and had an excess in the ASF account.

- Thirty-year service retirement
- Member is fifty-five years old at retirement
- Required amount = $90,000
- Member's ASF balance = $190,000

- Excess = $100,000
- Member's FAS = $120,000
- Earnings from twenty to thirty years = $1,100,000

Calculation:
- 50% of FAS = $60,000
- Value of 1/60 = $18,333
- ($1,100,000/60)
- Estimated value of NYC ITHP benefit = $8,247
- Value of excess = $9,376
- Annual pension = $95,956

Value of 1/60 Calculation

Calculating the value of the 1/60 benefit is quite simple. The starting point is to determine the total amount of earnings from after the twentieth anniversary until retirement. Technically, if an individual were to retire after 20 years and one day, the amount of money earned for that one day beyond 20 years would receive a 1/60 benefit. Once the total earnings are determined, divide by 60.

$$\frac{\text{Total earnings after twentieth anniversary}}{60}$$

Note: the 1/60 benefit continues until retirement; the thirty-year cap was removed by legislation in February 2002.

Value of Excess Pension Benefit Calculation

Calculating the value of an excess requires a little more math than the 1/60 calculation. To calculate the excess benefit, the pre-retiree Police Pension Fund member would need to know the following information: excess value (total ASF balance less required amount) and an annuity factor based on age. The required amount and the excess can be obtained from a member's NYC Police Pension Fund Annual Pension Statement. The annuity factor (or value based on each $1,000 of excess) can be obtained from Table #4 on the following page:

Table #4	
Age at retirement	**Per $1,000**
40	78.44
41	79.03
42	79.64
43	80.31
44	81.02
45	81.78
46	82.60
47	83.48
48	84.43
49	85.46
50	86.57
51	87.79
52	89.11
53	90.56
54	92.10
55	93.76
56	95.52
57	97.41
58	99.44
59	101.64
60	104.04
61	106.66
62	109.52
63	112.66

The following is an example of the pension value of an excess calculation.

- Excess amount = $60,000
- Age at retirement = 50

Calculation:
- Excess amount/1000 × 86.57
- $60,000/1000 × 86.57
- Excess pension benefit value = $5,194

Value of NYC ITHP Pension Benefit Calculation

Police Pension Fund members who retire (service retirement) with more than twenty years of service receive this added pension benefit. An individual who is granted a three-quarter accidental disability pension will receive the benefit even if twenty years of service is not completed. This calculation is more involved, and it may be easier for a pre-retiree to estimate this benefit when planning for retirement. To estimate the NYC ITHP pension benefit the pre-retiree Police Pension Fund member would need to know the following information: earnings from the twentieth anniversary until retirement (for a service retirement), the NYC ITHP contribution rate, the interest rate factor, and the annuity factor. Currently, the NYC ITHP contribution rate is 5%, the interest rate earned is 8.25%, and the same annuity factors in Table #4 are used. The following is an example of an *estimated* NYC ITHP pension benefit calculation.

- Twenty-two-year service retirement
- Age at retirement = 45
- Earnings twenty-first year = $110,000
- Earnings twenty-second year = $115,000

Calculation:

- $110,000 × .05 = $5,500
- $5,500 × 1.0825 + $5,750 = $11,704
- $11,704/1000 × 81.78 = $957
- Value of estimated NYC ITHP pension benefit = $957

Twenty vs. Twenty-Five vs. Thirty Year Service Retirement

As Police Pension Fund members get close to twenty years of service, they often ask about the benefit of staying to twenty-five years of service. In most cases, there is a significant monetary difference between a twenty year pension and a twenty-five year pension. In order to complete an analysis of twenty vs. twenty-five vs. thirty year retirements, pre-retirees need to make some assumptions about their projected earnings and pension contributions. The following lengthy example will attempt to show the difference between a twenty-year pension, a twenty-five-year pension, and a thirty-year pension.

Twenty-Year Service Retirement Pension

- Twenty years of service
- Forty-five years old
- FAS = $110,000
- Required amount = $90,000
- Member's ASF balance = $125,000
- Excess = $35,000

Calculation:

- 50% of FAS = $55,000
- Value of excess = $2,862
- Total annual pension benefit after 20 years = $57,862

Twenty-Five-Year Service Retirement Pension

- Assumption of 1% FAS increase per year
- ($111,100, $112,211, $113,333, $114,466, & $115,611)
- Assumption of an additional $2,000 to FAS based on longevity
- Assumption that member elected the ITHP waiver for the entire five-year period
- Twenty-five years of service
- Fifty years old
- FAS = $117,611
- Required amount = $90,000
- Member's ASF balance = $233,505
- Excess = $143,505

Calculation:

- 50% of FAS = $58,806
- Value of 1/60 = $9,445
- ($566,721/60)
- Estimated value of NYC ITHP benefit = $2,888
- Value of excess = $12,423
- Total annual pension benefit after twenty-five years = $83,562

Thirty-Year Service Retirement Pension

- Assumption of 1% FAS increase per year
  ($118,787, $119,975, $121,175, $122,386, & $123,610)
- Assumption that member elected the ITHP waiver for the entire five-year period
- Thirty years of service
- Fifty-five years old
- FAS = $123,610

- Required amount = $90,000
- Member's ASF balance = $398,092
- Excess = $308,092

Calculation:
- 50% of FAS = $61,805
- Value of 1/60 = $19,544
  ($1,172,654/60)
- Estimated value of NYC ITHP benefit = $6,232
- Value of excess = $28,887
- Total annual pension benefit after thirty years = $116,468

Next, the pre-retiree would need to analyze the length of time it would take to make up not receiving the pension benefit at twenty years—also known as a breakeven point. The breakeven point is the point at which you would have received the same total amount of money from the Police Pension Fund no matter when you retired. Many retirees do a similar calculation when deciding whether to take a Social Security retirement benefit at sixty-two years old or to delay to a later age. Using the figures from the example, Table #5 displays the result.

Table #5			
Age	20 Year Retirement	25 Year Retirement	30 Year Retirement
46	$57,862	$0	$0
47	$57,862	$0	$0
48	$57,862	$0	$0
49	$57,862	$0	$0
50	$57,862	$0	$0
51	$57,862	$83,562	$0
52	$57,862	$83,562	$0
53	$57,862	$83,562	$0
54	$57,862	$83,562	$0
55	$57,862	$83,562	$0
56	$57,862	$83,562	$116,468
57	$57,862	$83,562	$116,468
58	$57,862	$83,562	$116,468
59	$57,862	$83,562	$116,468
60	$57,862	$83,562	$116,468
61	$57,862	$83,562	$116,468
Total received	$925,792	$919,182	$698,808
62	$57,862	$83,562	$116,468
63	$57,862	$83,562	$116,468
64	$57,862	$83,562	$116,468
65	$57,862	$83,562	$116,468
Total received	$1,157,240	$1,253,430	$1,164,680
66	$57,862	$83,562	$116,468
67	$57,862	$83,562	$116,468
68	$57,862	$83,562	$116,468
Total received	$1,330,826	$1,504,116	$1,514,084

Table #6			
Summary of 20 vs. 25 vs. 30 example			
	20 Year Retirement	25 Year Retirement	30 Year Retirement
Annual pension benefit	$57,862	$83,562	$116,468
Percentage increase	N/A	44%	40%
Retirement age	45	50	55
Breakeven point (age) vs. 20 yr. retirement	N/A	61	65
Breakeven point (age) vs. 25 yr. retirement	N/A	N/A	68

The example shows that remaining on the job until twenty-five years of service resulted in an approximately 44% larger annual pension benefit than the twenty-year retirement. The length of time to make up the difference of staying until twenty-five years of service was a little over eleven years. In other words, the twenty-five-year pension begins to surpass the twenty-year pension after the eleventh or twelfth year of retirement. The thirty-year retirement resulted in an approximately 40% larger annual pension benefit than the twenty-five-year retirement and an approximately 101% larger annual pension benefit than the twenty-year retirement. The length of time to make up the difference of staying until thirty years of service was about thirteen years when compared with the twenty-five-year retirement and about ten years when compared with the twenty-year retirement. Determining the breakeven point should not be the only criteria when an individual is trying to decide whether to retire after twenty years of service. Other factors to consider may include job satisfaction, life expectancy, overall health, interest earned on ASF account, desire for a second career, etc.

Pension Loan

Police Pension Fund members with more than three years of service are permitted to borrow money from their pension account (ASF). Prior to electing to take a pension loan, the member should carefully review the related rules in order to prevent taxability. This is one area where a member can easily make a mistake, and very often, the mistake is irrevocable or difficult to fix. Ideally, members should not take a pension loan during their careers in order to receive the highest pension benefit possible at retirement. Of course, the ideal is not the reality for most members, and a pension loan becomes a necessity at some point as a result of unexpected expenses, family financial obligations, etc. Prior to requesting a pension loan, a member may want to review any other available methods to receive the needed funds. For example, it may make more sense for a member to finance the purchase of a new car using a car dealer's low financing rates rather than taking a pension loan. A significant disadvantage of taking a pension loan is that the monies removed no longer receive the 8.25% rate of return for funds in a member's ASF account. As many members are aware, taking a pension loan(s) results in a shortage, and if not corrected through the ITHP waiver and/or 50% additional results in a reduced pension at retirement. The following are a few factors to take into account when taking a pension loan:

- Are other loan sources available? Home equity, family, NYC Deferred Compensation Plan, etc.?
- Is there "tax-free" money available from the member's ASF account? Removing the tax-free money, whether it is a loan or a distribution, still results in the money no longer earning the 8.25% rate of return.
- If a member borrows taxable contributions and the repayment schedule is greater than five years, the loan becomes taxable and may be subject to a 10% penalty. The 10% penalty is assessed for a member who is less than fifty-nine and one-half years old.
- If a member borrows tax-free money, the repayment schedule can be longer than five years if desired. No taxable distribution is applied when borrowing tax-free money.
- Carefully complete the Police Pension Fund Loan Application form. If you are not sure about something on the form, ask someone at the Police Pension Fund.

There is an IRS Internal Revenue Code exception available to the five-year repayment schedule for taxable pension loans. This exception may allow a participant to extend the five-year repayment schedule when purchasing a primary residence. For members considering this exception, it is strongly recommended that you consult a qualified and knowledgeable tax professional. Incorrectly using this exception may result in IRS scrutiny (audit).

Final Distribution (final loan)

At retirement, Police Pension Fund members will have to decide whether to elect to take a final distribution (often referred to as the final loan) from their ASF account. Members often have great difficulty determining what is best for their situation.

Very simply, electing to receive the final distribution results in a lower pension benefit, and not electing to receive the final distribution results in a higher pension benefit. How much a member's pension decreases or increases is based on various factors, such as appointment date, age at retirement, and type of money removed. The retiring member has the option to receive a full final distribution or a partial final distribution. A full final distribution would amount to 90% of the required amount and any excess funds available (including tax free). A partial final distribution would amount to a portion of the required amount, a portion of the excess, tax-free only, excess only, etc.

Final Distribution Calculation Examples

Example #1 is a basic calculation of a retiring member who has elected to take the full final distribution.

- Twenty-year service retirement
- Forty-five years old at retirement
- Appointment date after August 1985
- FAS = $110,000
- Required amount = $90,000
- Member's ASF account = $125,000
- Member's excess amount = $35,000
- Full final distribution available = $116,000

Calculation:
- 50% of FAS = $55,000

- Value of excess = $2,862
  ($35,000/1000 × 81.78)
- Annual pension benefit before full final distribution = $57,862
  ($55,000 + 2,862)
- Annual pension benefit reduced by full final distribution = $9,486
  ($116,000/1000 × 81.78)
- Annual pension benefit after full final distribution =
  $48,376 ($57,862 - 9,486)
- Annual pension benefit received is 44% of FAS

Note: If the member in the above example decided to elect a partial final distribution of only the excess funds, the annual pension benefit would be equal to 50% of the FAS.

Example #2 is a retiring member who has a significant excess and has elected to take the full final distribution.

- Thirty-year service retirement
- Fifty-five years old at retirement
- Appointment date before August 1985
- FAS = $150,000
- Required amount = $120,000
- Earnings from twenty to thirty service years = $1,100,000
- Member's ASF account = $325,000
- Member's excess amount = $205,000
- Full final distribution available = $313,000

Calculation:
- 50% of FAS = $75,000

- Value of 1/60 = $18,333
- ($1,100,000/60)
- Estimated value of NYC ITHP benefit = $9,000
- Value of excess =$19,221
- ($205,000/1000 × 93.76)
- Total annual pension benefit before full final distribution = $121,544 ($75,000 + 18,333 + 9,000 + 19,221)
- Annual pension benefit reduced by full final distribution =
  1. 90% of required amount/1000 × 75.21 = $8,123
  2. Excess amount/1000 × 93.76 = $19,221
     $27,344 ($8,123 + 19,221)
- Annual pension benefit after full final distribution = $94,200 ($121,544 − 27,344)
- Annual pension benefit received is 63% of FAS

Example #3 is a retiring member (using the same dollar figures as example #2) who has a significant excess and has elected to take a partial final distribution of the excess funds only.

- Thirty-year service retirement
- Fifty-five years old at retirement
- Appointment date before August 1985
- FAS = $150,000
- Required amount = $120,000
- Earnings from twenty to thirty service years = $1,100,000
- Member's ASF account = $325,000
- Member's excess amount = $205,000
- Full final distribution available = $313,000

Calculation:

- 50% of FAS = $75,000
- Value of 1/60 = $18,333
  ($1,100,000/60)
- Estimated value of NYC ITHP benefit = $9,000
- Value of excess = $19,221
  ($205,000/1000 × 93.76)
- Total annual pension benefit before full final distribution = $121,544 ($75,000 + 18,333 + 9,000 + 19,221)
- Annual pension benefit reduced by partial final distribution = $19,221 ($205,000/1000 × 93.76)
- Annual pension benefit after partial final distribution = $102,323 ($121,544 − 19,221)
- Annual pension benefit received is 68% of FAS

Final Distribution Advantages and Disadvantages

When a retiring member elects to take a final distribution, the funds withdrawn become the member's personal asset. Since the retiring member now owns the funds, he or she has the ability to spend and/or invest it as desired (there are various income tax rules regarding the final distribution, which will be reviewed later). As previously reviewed, electing a final distribution results in a lower annual pension benefit. This lower annual pension benefit continues throughout the life of the retiree and beneficiary, if applicable.

For a member who does not elect a final distribution, the NYC Police Pension Fund keeps the money, interest is no longer credited to the member, and the member no longer has access to or ownership of the money. Not electing the final distribution results in a larger annual pension benefit for the life of the retiree and beneficiary, if applicable.

Electing a final distribution affords the retiree the opportunity to earn interest/appreciation on the withdrawn funds. The appreciation of the withdrawn funds is critical because the true purchasing power of the annual pension benefit received will become significantly reduced as the retiree ages. Currently, Police Pension Fund retirees receive a small cost-of-living adjustment (COLA) after certain conditions are met. The COLA, 50% of CPI, is only based on the first $18,000 of pension benefit and has a minimum of 1% and a maximum of 3%. Therefore, the minimum COLA adjustment is $180 per year and the maximum is $540 per year. Because of the limited COLA, the annual pension benefit will not keep pace with inflation over a retiree's lifetime. For example, a retiree who receives an annual pension benefit of $50,000 may begin to realize the significant effects of inflation erosion five to ten years after retirement. Five years after retirement, a $50,000 annual pension benefit will be worth $44,193, based on an inflation factor of 2.5%. Ten years after retirement, the $50,000 annual pension benefit will be worth $39,060, based on an inflation factor of 2.5%. Obviously, if a retiree lives through a period of high inflation, the true purchasing power of the annual pension benefit will become even more reduced.

Rolling Over the Final Distribution

This is another topic that some pre-retirees have difficulty in understanding and properly executing. Ideally, a member that elects the final distribution will rollover the taxable portion of the final distribution (in order to prevent immediate taxation) into a new retirement plan. The general rule regarding distributions from the new retirement plan is that distributions are taxable and subject to a 10% penalty if received prior to fifty-nine and one-half years old (there are exceptions to the 10% penalty). If a member decides to not rollover the taxable portion of the final distribution it will be considered a taxable distribution and will be subject to tax and a 10% penalty if less than fifty-years old at retirement. Table # 7 summarizes.

Table #7			
	Age at retirement	10% penalty	Taxable
Not rolling over taxable final distribution	Less than 50	Yes	Yes
Not rolling over taxable final distribution	50 and over	No	Yes
Rolling over the taxable final distribution	Any age	No	No
Distributions from new retirement plan	N/A	Yes, if less than 59 ½ years old (exceptions)	Yes, in most cases

Rolling Over to a New Retirement Plan

The next question is what type of a retirement plan the taxable final distribution can be rolled into. This is also another difficult decision for many pre-retirees because of the number of choices and the process of rolling over the money. Two methods are available for rolling over the final distribution. The first method is a direct rollover from the Police Pension Fund into a new retirement plan. The direct rollover occurs at retirement after correctly completing the paperwork provided by the Police Pension Fund. The second method is a direct payment to the retiring member. For a member who elects the direct payment method, 20% is withheld from the check(s) for taxes. In order to avoid taxation, the taxable final distribution money must be rolled into the new retirement plan within sixty days of the date(s) of the check(s) received from the Police Pension Fund. Prior to rolling over the money, the retiree should make copies of the checks. The copies of the checks should be retained in a folder that the retiree maintains for important tax/financial documents. In most cases, direct rollover is the preferred method for members who choose to elect the final distribution.

The retiring member will need to decide what type of retirement plan into which to rollover the taxable final distribution. Selecting which retirement plan is best depends on various factors: personal preferences, investing knowledge, risk tolerance, etc. Currently, the following retirement plans are available for the rollover of the taxable final distribution.

- Individual retirement account (IRA)
- Roth Individual Retirement Account (Roth IRA)
- NYC Deferred Compensation Plan Pension Rollover Account
- Union-sponsored annuity plan (in some cases)
- New employer retirement plan

Individual Retirement Account

The IRA may be an option for the retiree who desires a large number of investment choices and types and/or for the retiree who is seeking the safety of certificates of deposit (CDs). An IRA can be established at a bank, a discount brokerage firm (Charles Schwab, Scottrade, etc.), or through a financial advisor. Many are not aware that IRAs can be invested in different types of securities or financial products. An IRA may be invested in mutual funds, individual equities (stocks), CDs, bonds, etc. Depending on where the IRA is established, the retiree may have the ability to choose among thousands of investments.

Roth Individual Retirement Account

The Roth IRA has the same type of investing flexibility and custodian choices of the IRA. The difference between an IRA and a Roth IRA is the tax implications of rolling over the money. Correctly rolling over the taxable final distribution money into an IRA will result in not owing any taxes; the retiree is simply deferring the taxes. Alternatively, there is a current taxable event if the retiree rolls over the taxable final distribution into a Roth IRA. How much taxes would be owed depends on numerous factors: value of the taxable final distribution, the retiree's tax bracket, type of retirement (service or accidental), etc. Table #8 compares rolling over the taxable final distribution into an IRA vs. a Roth IRA.

Table #8		
	IRA	**Roth IRA**
Taxable final distribution	$100,000	$100,000
W2 earnings prior to retirement	$75,000	$75,000
Pension benefit from retirement to year end	$30,000	$30,000
Itemized deduction for the year	$20,000	$20,000
Filing status	Single	Single
Exemption	$3,800	$3,800
Taxable income	$81,200	$181,200
Tax bracket (2012)	25%	33%

As Table #8 indicates, rolling over the taxable final distribution into a Roth IRA increased the retiree's tax bracket to 33%. For a retiree considering the Roth IRA, it may be worthwhile to meet with a qualified tax/financial advisor in order to fully understand the tax implications for the retiree's particular situation. The advantages of a Roth IRA will be reviewed in a later chapter.

NYC Deferred Compensation Plan Pension Rollover Account

The NYC Deferred Compensation Plan offers an account that allows Police Pension Fund members to rollover their taxable final distribution at retirement. The money rolled over would be put into a separate account and is not comingled with any other NYC Deferred Compensation Plan accounts the member may have. The purpose of not comingling the accounts is to keep track of the original New York State (NYS) tax basis when the funds were rolled over. This may be a suitable option for the retiree who likes familiarity. Many Police Pension Fund members have participated in the NYC Deferred Compensation Plan for years and are very familiar with the variety of investment choices offered.

Union-Sponsored Annuity Plan

In some cases, the retiring member may be able to rollover the taxable final distribution into a union-sponsored annuity plan. Many members pay little attention to their union sponsored annuity plans while working, but this is an option available at retirement. The retiring member should check with his or her own union to determine whether this option is available.

New Employer Retirement Plan

For the retiree moving on to a new employer, the taxable final distribution may be rolled over into the new employer's retirement plan. The new employer's retirement plan would have to permit incoming rollovers, and the type of the new employer's plan would also have to be reviewed. Additionally, the retiree would also have to review the investment choices offered in the new employer plan and determine if those choices are suitable for the retiree's overall financial situation.

Appreciation of the Rollover Account

As reviewed earlier, the main purpose of electing the final distribution is to invest the money in order to attempt to keep up with or surpass the rate of inflation. This is a task that many police retirees have difficulty in achieving. The selection of an appropriate investment(s) should be based on a retiree's overall risk tolerance, time horizon, purpose of money, etc. A tremendous amount of information (too much) is available to assist the retiree in selecting an appropriate investment for his or her particular situation. What type of investment(s) to select is beyond the scope of this book. Electing the final distribution and investing it prudently is not a get rich scheme and requires discipline and investing prowess. Quite simply, the retiree has two choices: do it on your own or hire an investment professional. Retirees who want to invest on their own should read a basic investing book or take an adult-education course on the principles of investing money. Hiring an investment professional will be reviewed in a later chapter.

Table #9 shows how a rollover account would appreciate using different rates of return.

Table #9				
Taxable Final Distribution Rolled Over = $100,000				
Years retired	Value at 2% appreciation	Value at 4% appreciation	Value at 6% appreciation	Value at 8% appreciation
1	$102,000	$104,000	$106,000	$108,000
2	104,040	108,160	$112,360	$116,640
3	106,121	112,486	$119,102	$125,971
4	108,243	116,986	$126,248	$136,049
5	110,408	121,665	$133,823	$146,933
6	112,614	126,532	$141,852	$158,687
7	114,869	131,593	$150,363	$171,382
8	117,166	136,857	$159,385	$185,093
9	119,509	142,331	$168,948	$199,900
10	121,899	148,024	$179,085	$215,892
11	124,337	153,945	$189,830	$233,164
12	126,824	160,103	$201,220	$251,817
13	129,361	166,507	$213,293	$271,962
14	131,948	173,168	$226,090	$293,719
15	134,587	180,094	$239,656	$317,217
16	137,279	187,298	$254,035	$342,594
17	140,024	194,790	$269,277	$370,002
18	142,825	202,582	$285,434	$399,602
19	145,681	210,685	$302,560	$431,570
20	$148,595	$219,112	$320,714	$466,096

Comparing Final Distribution vs. No Final Distribution

When analyzing the final distribution decision, many pre-retirees calculate how long after NYPD retirement they will have to live to make up the "cost" of the final distribution. The calculation they perform is simply the total final distribution divided by the cost of the final distribution. For example, if a retiree elects a $150,000 final distribution and the cost is $12,267, it would take the retiree a little over twelve years to "be ahead of the game." Although this is an easy calculation to perform and understand, it may not be accurate when compared to electing the final distribution and the appreciation of the final distribution. Additionally, the retiree would probably spend the increased pension benefit, resulting in a reduction of overall wealth.

Another question that a retiree often asks is how many years it will take to make more in appreciation than what the final distribution cost. Table #10 displays, based on a forty-five year old retiree, how long it takes to actually earn more in appreciation than the cost of the final distribution.

Table #10			
Taxable Final Distribution Rolled Over = $150,000			
"Cost" of Final Distribution = $12,267			
Years retired	At 2% appreciation	At 4% appreciation	At 5% appreciation	At 6% appreciation
---	---	---	---	---
1	$3,000	$6,000	$7,500	$9,000
2	3,060	6,240	7,875	9,540
3	3,121	6,490	8,269	10,112
4	3,184	6,749	8,682	10,719
5	3,247	7,019	9,116	11,362
6	3,312	7,300	9,572	12,044
7	3,378	7,592	10,051	**12,767**
8	3,446	7,896	10,553	13,533
9	3,515	8,211	11,081	14,345
10	3,585	8,540	11,635	15,205
11	3,657	8,881	12,217	16,118
12	3,730	9,237	**12,828**	17,085
13	3,805	9,606	13,469	18,110
14	3,881	9,990	14,142	19,196
15	3,958	10,390	14,849	20,348
16	4,038	10,806	15,592	21,569
17	4,118	11,238	16,372	22,863
18	4,201	11,687	17,190	24,235
19	4,285	12,155	18,050	25,689
20	$4,370	**$12,641**	$18,952	$27,230

A review of Table #10 indicates that a retiree investing in a rollover account, assuming a 6% appreciation rate, would take approximately seven years after retirement to earn more money than the cost of the final distribution. A 5% appreciation rate would take approximately twelve years, and at 4%, approximately twenty years would be necessary. Believe it or not, if a retiree were to assume a 2% appreciation rate, it would take over seventy years.

Taking this analysis a step further, Table #11 compares electing the final distribution vs. not electing the final distribution, when taxes are taken into account. For the retiree who does not elect the final distribution, gross income increases because of the higher annual pension benefit. This higher gross income normally results in more current taxes owed. For the retiree who elects the final distribution, the funds are rolled into a retirement plan and the appreciation of the account is tax deferred.

Table #11				
Taxable Final Distribution Rolled Over = $150,000				
"Cost" of Final Distribution = $12,267				
Assumed rate of appreciation = 5%				
Tax rate = 20% federal				
Years retired	At 5% appreciation	After-tax "cost" of final distribution	Gain or loss	Cumulative
1	$7,500	$9,814	($2,314)	($2,314)
2	7,875	9,814	(1,939)	(4,253)
3	8,269	9,814	(1,545)	(5,798)
4	8,682	9,814	(1,132)	(6,930)
5	9,116	9,814	(698)	(7,628)
6	9,572	9,814	(242)	(7,870)
7	10,051	9,814	237	(7,633)
8	10,553	9,814	739	(6,894)
9	11,081	9,814	1,267	(5,627)
10	11,635	9,814	1,821	(3,806)
11	12,217	9,814	2,403	(1,403)
12	12,828	9,814	3,014	**1,611**
13	13,469	9,814	3,655	5,266
14	14,142	9,814	4,328	9,594
15	14,849	9,814	5,035	14,629
16	15,592	9,814	5,778	20,407
17	16,372	9,814	6,558	26,965
18	17,190	9,814	7,376	34,341
19	18,050	9,814	8,236	42,577
20	$18,952	$9,814	9,138	$51,715

As Table #11 indicates, beginning at the end of the first year retired, the retiree who selected the final distribution would be at a $2,314 loss, based on the assumptions. At the end of retirement year seven, the retiree begins to see a gain on the final distribution rollover account vs. the after-tax cost of the final distribution. Then, at the end of retirement year twelve, the cumulative column turns positive.

Summary: Final Distribution vs. No Final Distribution

Table #12		
	Final distribution	No final distribution
Annual pension benefit	Reduced	Increased
Current income tax	Reduced	Increased
Ownership of funds	Retiree	Police Pension Fund
Accessibility of funds	Yes	No
Opportunity to appreciate	Yes	No
Select a beneficiary	Yes	No

Ordinary Disability Pension

The ordinary disability pension is granted to a retiree who suffers an illness or injury that is not considered in the line of duty. A Police Pension Fund member who retires with an ordinary disability pension does not receive the annual Variable Supplement Fund (VSF) payment and does not receive any VSF Deferred Retirement Option Plan (DROP) payment, if applicable. In addition, an ordinary disability pension is taxed by the federal government.

The basic annual ordinary disability pension benefit is calculated as follows:

Twenty or more years of service
- 1/40 for every year of service × FAS
- Plus annuity value of the excess over the required amount or less the annuity value of a shortage

More than ten, but less than twenty years of service
- 50% of FAS
- Plus annuity value of the excess over the required amount or less the annuity value of a shortage

Less than ten years of service
- 33 1/3% of FAS
- Plus annuity value of the excess over the required amount or less the annuity value of a shortage

Ordinary Disability Pension Calculations

Example #1 is a basic calculation of a retiring ordinary disability member who has elected not to take the full final distribution.

- Twenty-two-year ordinary disability retirement
- Member is forty-four years old at retirement
- Required amount = $90,000
- Member's ASF balance = $125,000
- Excess = $35,000

- Final distribution = No
- Member's FAS = $110,000

Calculation:
- 1/40 × years of service x FAS
- .025 × 22 × 110,000 = $60,500
- Annuity value of excess = $2,996
  (35,000/1000 × 85.6)
- Annual pension benefit = $63,496

Example #2 is a basic calculation of a retiring ordinary disability member who has elected to take the full final distribution.

- Twenty-two-year ordinary disability retirement
- Member is forty-four years old at retirement
- Required amount = $90,000
- Member's ASF balance = $125,000
- Excess = $35,000
- Final distribution = Yes
- Member's FAS = $110,000

Calculation:
- 1/40 x years of service x FAS
- .025 × 22 × 110,000 = $60,500
- Annuity value of excess = $2,996
  (35,000/1000 × 85.6)
- Annual pension benefit before final distribution = $63,496
- Less annuity value of excess = $2,996
- Less annuity value of 90% of required amount = $6,934

- Annual pension benefit after final distribution = $53,566
  (63,496 − 2,996 − 6,934)

Accidental Disability Pension

An accidental disability pension is granted to a member who is determined to be physically or mentally unable to perform as a NYC Police Officer. The disability is a result of an accidental injury in the line of duty. A Police Pension Fund member who retires with an accidental disability pension does not receive the annual VSF payment and does not receive any VSF DROP payment, if applicable. The tax implications of an accidental disability changed on January 1, 2009, and have caused some confusion among accidental disability pension members.

Accidental Disability Pension Tax Issues

Prior to January 1, 2009, a Police Pension Fund accidental disability pension benefit was federally tax-free. After January 1, 2009 members retiring with an accidental disability pension benefit will have some of their benefit taxed by the federal government. How much will be taxed depends on total years of service, final or no final distribution, and other factors. The following items are subject to federal tax in reference to an accidental disability pension:

1. Value of 1/60 benefit
2. Annuity value of ASF balance if no final distribution
3. Annuity value of 10% required amount if final distribution elected
4. NYC ITHP benefit after 20 years of service

Accidental Disability Pension Calculations

Example #1 is a basic calculation of a retiring accidental disability member who has elected not to take the full final distribution.

- Ten-year accidental disability retirement
- Member is forty-one years old at retirement
- Required amount = $15,000
- 10% of required amount = $1,500
- Member's ASF balance = $50,000
- Final distribution = No
- Member's FAS = $90,000

Calculation:
- 75% × FAS
- .75 × 90,000 = $67,500
- Annuity value of ASF = $3,977
- (48,500/1000 × 82.0)
- Estimated value of NYC ITHP benefit = $2,500
- Annual pension benefit = $73,977
  ($67,500 + 3,977 + 2,500)

Federal tax:
- Annuity value of ASF = $3,977
- 10% of required amount value = $120
- Estimated annual pension subject to federal tax = $4,097
  ($3,977 + 120)
- Annual pension not subject to federal tax = $69,880

Example #2 is a basic calculation of a retiring accidental disability member (using the same dollar figures as example 1) who has elected to take the full final distribution.

- Ten-year accidental disability retirement
- Member is forty-one years old at retirement
- Required amount = $15,000
- 10% of required amount = $1,500
- Member's ASF balance = $50,000
- Final distribution = Yes
- Member's FAS = $90,000

Calculation:
- 75% x FAS
- .75 x 90,000 = $67,500
- Annuity value of ASF = $3,977
- (48,500/1000 × 82.0)
- Estimated value of NYC ITHP benefit = $2,500
- Annual pension benefit before final distribution = $73,977 ($67,500 + 3,977 + 2,500)
- Annual pension benefit after final distribution = $70,000 ($73,977 − 3,977)

Federal tax:
- 10% of required amount value = $120
- Estimated annual pension subject to federal tax = $120
- Annual pension not subject to federal tax = $69,880

Example #3 is a calculation of a retiring accidental disability member who has elected to not take the full final distribution.

- Twenty-five-year accidental disability retirement
- Member is forty-eight years old at retirement
- Required amount = $130,000
- 10% of required amount = $13,000
- Member's ASF balance = $200,000
- Final distribution = No
- Earnings from twenty to twenty-five service years = $500,000
- Member's FAS = $120,000

Calculation:
- 75% × FAS
- .75 × 120,000 = $90,000
- Value of 1/60 = $8,333
- ($500,000/60)
- Annuity value of ASF = $16,849
- (187,000/1000 × 90.1)
- Estimated value of NYC ITHP benefit = $11,250
- Annual pension benefit= $126,432
  ($90,000 + $8,333+ 16,849 + 11,250)

Federal tax:
- Value of 1/60 = $8,333
- Annuity value of ASF = $16,849
- 10% of required amount value = $1,170
- Estimated value of NYC ITHP benefit after twenty years = $3,000

- Estimated annual pension subject to federal tax = $29,352
  ($8,333 + 16,849 + 1,170 + 3,000)
- Annual pension not subject to federal tax = $97,080

Example #4 is a calculation of a retiring accidental disability member (using the same dollar figures as example 3) who has elected to take the full final distribution.

- Twenty-five-year accidental disability retirement
- Member is forty-eight years old at retirement
- Required amount = $130,000
- 10% of required amount = $13,000
- Member's ASF balance = $200,000
- Final distribution = Yes
- Earnings from twenty to twenty-five service years = $500,000
- Member's FAS = $120,000

Calculation:
- 75% × FAS
- .75 × 120,000 = $90,000
- Value of 1/60 = $8,333
  ($500,000/60)
- Annuity value of ASF = $16,849
  (187,000/1000 × 90.1)
- Estimated value of NYC ITHP benefit = $11,250
- Annual pension benefit before final distribution = $126,432
  ($90,000 + 8,333 + 16,849, 11,250)
- Annual pension benefit after final distribution = $109,583
  ($126,432 − 16,849)

Federal tax:

- Value of 1/60 = $8,333
- 10% of required amount value = $1,170
- Estimated value of NYC ITHP benefit after twenty years = $3,000
- Estimated annual pension subject to federal tax = $12,503 ($8,333 + 1,170 + 3,000)
- Annual pension not subject to federal tax = $97,080

Accidental Disability Pension Final Distribution vs. No Final Distribution

Police Pension Fund members receiving an accidental disability pension will have to decide whether to elect a final distribution. The concept is basically the same as the service retiree: rollover to defer taxation, appreciation of the rollover account, ownership of funds, etc. Significant tax and retirement planning opportunities may be available for the individual who receives an accidental disability pension and elects the final distribution.

Variable Supplement Fund

Very simply, if a Police Pension Fund member retires (service retirement) with twenty years of service or more, he or she will receive the annual Variable Supplement Fund (VSF) payment. Currently, the VSF annual payment is $12,000 and is distributed to service retirees only; ordinary and accidental retirees do not receive the VSF annual benefit.

The VSF annual payment is taxed by the federal government but not by New York State.

VSF Deferred Retirement Option Plan (DROP)

The Variable Supplement Fund Deferred Retirement Option Plan (VSF DROP) became effective on January 1, 2002. The VSF DROP, also referred to as "banked VSF," is beneficial to the Police Pension Fund member who decides to stay on the job past twenty years of service. Prior to 2002, the Police Pension Fund member who decided to remain on the job after twenty years of service forfeited the annual VSF payment. Now, once twenty years of service is reached and the member does not retire, the VSF begins to get "banked."

Upon retirement, the Police Pension Fund member will need to decide what to do with the VSF DROP money. Basically, there are two choices: roll it over or distribute it. For most, the best choice would be to rollover the funds in order to avoid immediate taxation and a penalty, if applicable. The VSF DROP money has the same tax consequences as the final distribution, as shown in Table #13.

Table #13			
	Age at retirement	10% penalty	Taxable
Not rolling over VSF DROP	Less than 50	Yes	Yes
Not rolling over VSF DROP	50 and over	No	Yes
Rolling over the VSF DROP	Any age	No	No
Distributions from new retirement plan	N/A	Yes, if less than 59 ½ years old (exceptions)	Yes, in most cases

The VSF DROP money also has the same rollover options as the final distribution. VSF DROP money can be rolled over to the following:

- IRA
- Roth Individual Retirement Account (Roth IRA)
- NYC Deferred Compensation Plan Pension Rollover Account
- Union-sponsored annuity plan (in some cases)
- New employer retirement plan

Once the VSF DROP money is rolled over to the new retirement plan, it will be subject to the distribution rules of the new retirement plan. For example, assume a fifty-one year old Police Pension Fund member retires and rolls over the VSF DROP to an IRA and the following year takes a distribution from the IRA. In this case, the member would be subject to the 10% early withdrawal penalty.

Summary: Service, Ordinary, and Accidental Pension Benefits

Table #14			
	Service	Ordinary	Accidental
Annual VSF	Yes	No	No
VSF DROP	Yes	No	No
60ths	Yes	No	Yes
NYC ITHP benefit	Yes	No	Yes
Federal tax	Yes	Yes	Yes & No
NYS tax	No	No	No

Pension Options

Whether or not to select a pension option is a difficult decision for many Police Pension Fund retirees. Generally, the decision is made at finalization and is irrevocable. Finalization occurs when the NYC Chief Actuary is able to determine the final pension amount and the costs of the various options. Deciding to elect an option is based on many factors: personal choice, insurability, overall health, option cost, etc. Accidental disability retirees should carefully analyze the selection of an option because of the favorable tax treatment available to a beneficiary(ies). The following provides a brief summary of the available options:

- No option (maximum retirement allowance)
  -pension ends upon death of retiree
  -beneficiary receives nothing
- Option 2 (100% joint & survivor)
  -retiree receives reduced annual pension benefit
  -beneficiary receives 100% of reduced annual pension benefit
  -one beneficiary; cannot be changed
- Option 3 (50% joint & survivor)
  -retiree receives reduced annual pension benefit
  -beneficiary receives 50% of reduced annual pension benefit
  -one beneficiary; cannot be changed
- Option 4 (lump sum)
  -retiree receives reduced annual pension benefit
  -retiree elects a lump sum amount for beneficiary
  -more than one beneficiary can be designated and can be changed
- Option 4 (annuity)
  -retiree receives reduced annual pension benefit

-retiree elects an annuity amount for beneficiary

-one beneficiary; cannot be changed

- Option 5 (five-year certain)

    -retiree receives reduced annual pension benefit

    -if retiree dies within five years of retirement date, beneficiary receives pension until the fifth anniversary of retiree's retirement date

- Option 6 (ten-year certain)

    -retiree receives reduced annual pension benefit

    -if retiree dies before 10 years from retirement date, beneficiary receives pension until the tenth anniversary of retiree's retirement date

Note: There is also a "pop-up" feature offered with options 2, 3, and 4. The pop-up feature, if elected, allows the retiree's annual pension benefit to revert to the maximum retirement allowance if the beneficiary predeceases the retiree.

Tier III

Police Pension Fund members hired after June 30, 2009, and before April 1, 2012, were placed in Tier III. Police Pension Fund members with an appointment date of April 1, 2012 or after are placed in Tier III-revised. Even though Tier III has been in existence since the 1970s, it is new for Police Pension Fund members. Please note that the following is only an overview of Tier III benefits and is subject to revision. Tier III members should be guided by Police Pension Fund personnel and documents.

Table #15		
	Tier III	Tier III Revised
Appointment date	July 1st, 2009 to March 31st, 2012	April 1st, 2012 to the present
Pension contribution rate	3% of annual wages	3% of annual wages
Pension contributions	Not required after 25 years	Not required after 25 years
Interest rate earned on pension contributions	5.00%	5.00%
Pension loan(s)	No	No
Final average salary (FAS)	The greater of pensionable earnings of either average of final 36 months or average of three consecutive calendar years	Highest average wage earned in any consecutive five year period
Pensionable earnings limit	10%	10%
Social Security offset	Yes	Yes
Minimum vested requirement	5 years	5 years
Mandatory retirement age	62 years old	62 years old
VSF	Yes, after completion of 20 years	Yes, after completion of 20 years
VSF DROP	Yes, if not retired after 20 years	Yes, if not retired after 20 years

Basic Early Service Retirement

A Police Pension Fund Tier III member is eligible for an early service retirement after twenty years of service.

Formula:
- 2.1% × FAS × 20 years of service plus
- For every month beyond twenty years of service 0.33% of FAS (up to twenty-four months) less
- 50% of Social Security Retirement Benefit, commencing at age 62

Basic Normal Service Retirement

A Police Pension Fund member is eligible for a normal service retirement after twenty-two years of service.

Formula:
- 50% of FAS less
- 50% of Social Security Retirement Benefit commencing at age sixty-two

Note: The Social Security Retirement Benefit is calculated by only using the earnings while employed by the NYPD and other New York State public service employment, if applicable.

Escalation

The escalation provision of Tier III can be difficult to comprehend. Basically, the provision provides an additional benefit to most retiring members. On the basis of a number of factors, a member's annual pension benefit may increase a certain percentage each year. The increase can be defined as a reduced escalation or a full escalation.

The reduced escalation occurs when a Police Pension Fund member retires with less than twenty-five years of service (service retirement). Instead of receiving the full escalation, the member will receive a reduction of 1/36 of the full escalation for each month the member retired prior to the twenty-fifth anniversary. Example #1 is of a Police Pension Fund Tier III member who retires after twenty-two years of service and does not receive the escalation benefit.

- Twenty-two years of service
- Forty-five years old at retirement
- FAS = $130,000
- 50% of Social Security Retirement Benefit at 62 years old = $11,000

Calculation:
- 50% × FAS
- .50 × $130,000 = $65,000
- Less 50% of Social Security Retirement Benefit commencing at age 62 = $11,000
- Annual pension from forty-five years old until sixty-two years old = $65,000
- Annual pension from sixty-two years old until death = $54,000 ($65,000 − $11,000)

In the above example, the retired Tier III member did not receive any escalation benefit because the member retired with exactly twenty-two years of service. In order to receive the escalation benefit, the member could have continued working beyond twenty-two years or could have deferred the pension benefit.

Example #2 is of a Police Pension Fund Tier III member who retires after twenty-five years of service and is eligible for the full escalation.

- Twenty-five years of service
- Fifty years old at retirement
- FAS = $130,000
- 50% of Social Security Retirement Benefit at 62 years old = $11,000
- Assume 1.5% escalation rate

Calculation:
- 50% × FAS
- .50 × $130,000 = $65,000
- Less 50% of Social Security Retirement Benefit commencing at age 62 = $11,000
- Annual service retirement pension:
    1. At NYPD retirement = $65,000
    2. Retired one year = $65,975
    3. Retired two years = $66,965
    4. Retired three years = $67,969
    5. Retired four years = $68,989
    6. Retired five years = $70,023
    7. Retired six years = $71,074
    8. Retired seven years = $72,140
    9. Retired eight years = $73,222
    10. Retired nine years = $74,320

11. Retired ten years = $75,435

12. Retired eleven years = $76,567

13. Retired twelve years = $77,715 – $11,000 = $66,715
    (less 50% of Social Security Retirement Benefit at age 62)

14. Retired thirteen years = $78,881 – $11,000 = $67,881

15. Retired fourteen years = $80,064 – $11,000 =$69,064

16. Retired fifteen years = $81,265 – $11,000 = $70,265

In example #2 above, the retired member receives the full escalation upon retirement from the NYPD. The full escalation continues even after the reduction of 50% of the Social Security Retirement Benefit at age sixty-two.

Ordinary Disability Pension

The ordinary disability pension for a Tier III member is significantly different than a Tier II member. The most significant difference is that the Tier III member must also be eligible to receive Social Security disability benefits. In other words, the Tier III member must first be determined to be disabled by Social Security and then determined to be disabled by the NYPD Medical Board. The basic calculation to determine the ordinary disability benefit is the greater of the following:

- 33 1/3% of final average salary (FAS) or 2% of the FAS times years of credited service
- Reduced by 50% of the Social Security disability benefit

The following is an example of a Tier III member who has been determined to be disabled by both the Social Security Administration and by the NYPD Medical Board.

- Fifteen years of service
- Forty-five years old at retirement
- FAS = $130,000
- 50% of Social Security disability benefit at retirement =$12,000
- Assume 1.5% escalation rate

Calculation:

- 33 1/3% × FAS
- .3333 x $130,000 = $43,333
- Less 50% of Social Security disability benefit, commencing at retirement = $12,000
- Annual ordinary disability pension:
    1. At NYPD retirement = $43,333 – $12,000 = $31,333
    2. Retired one year = $43,983 – $12,000 = $31,983
    3. Retired two years = $44,643 – $12,000 = $32,643
    4. Retired three years = $45,313 – $12,000 = $33,313
    5. Retired four years = $45,993 – $12,000 = $33,993
    6. Retired five years = $46,683 – $12,000 = $34,683
    7. Retired six years = $47,383 – $12,000 = $35,383
    8. Retired seven years = $48,094 – $12,000 = $36,094
    9. Retired eight years = $48,815 – $12,000 = $36,815
    10. Retired nine years = $49,547 – $12,000 = $37,547
    11. Retired ten years = $50,290 – $12,000 = $38,290
    12. Retired eleven years = $51,044 – $12,000 = $39,044
    13. Retired twelve years = $51,810 – $12,000 = $39,810
    14. Retired thirteen years = $52,587 – $12,000 = $40,587
    15. Retired fourteen years = $53,376 – $12,000 =$41,376
    16. Retired fifteen years = $54,177 – $12,000 = $42,177

In the example above, the retired member receives the full escalation upon retirement from the NYPD. The NYPD ordinary disability pension is immediately reduced by 50% of the Social Security disability benefit.

Accidental Disability Pension

The accidental disability pension for a Tier III member is also significantly different than for a Tier II member. The most significant difference is that the Tier III member receives 50% of final average salary instead of the 75% received by Tier II members. The Tier III accidental disability pensioner does not have to be disabled by the Social Security Administration like the ordinary disability pensioner. The basic calculation to determine the accidental disability benefit is as follows:

- 50% of FAS
- Reduced by 50% of the Social Security disability benefit

The following is an example of a Tier III member who has been determined accidentally disabled by the NYPD Medical Board and will receive Social Security Disability benefits:

- Fifteen years of service
- Forty-five years old at retirement
- FAS = $130,000
- 50% of Social Security disability benefit at retirement = $12,000
- Assume 1.5% escalation rate

Calculation:
- 50% × FAS

- .50 × $130,000 = $65,000
- Less 50% of Social Security disability benefit commencing at retirement = $12,000
- Annual accidental disability pension:
    1. At NYPD retirement = $65,000 − $12,000 = $53,000
    2. Retired one year = $65,975 − $12,000 = $53,975
    3. Retired two years = $66,965 − $12,000 = $54,965
    4. Retired three years = $67,969 − $12,000 = $55,969
    5. Retired four years = $68,989 − $12,000 = $56,989
    6. Retired five years = $70,024 − $12,000 = $58,024
    7. Retired six years = $71,074 − $12,000 = $59,074
    8. Retired seven years = $72,140 − $12,000 = $60,140
    9. Retired eight years = $73,222 − $12,000 = $61,222
    10. Retired nine years = $74,320 − $12,000 = $62,320
    11. Retired ten years = $75,435 − $12,000 = $63,435
    12. Retired eleven years = $76,567 − $12,000 = $64,567
    13. Retired twelve years = $77,715 − $12,000 = $65,715
    14. Retired thirteen years = $78,881 − $12,000 = $66,881
    15. Retired fourteen years = $80,064 − $12,000 =$68,064
    16. Retired fifteen years = $81,265 − $12,000 = $69,265

In the example above, the retired member receives the full escalation upon retirement from the NYPD. The NYPD accidental disability pension is immediately reduced by 50% of the Social Security disability benefit.

Chapter 1: Summary

Retiring from the NYPD is a difficult decision and should be based on an individual's personal situation. Before retiring, the NYPD Police Pension member should fully understand both the advantages and disadvantages of retiring after twenty years of service vs. remaining on the job. Of course, retiring after twenty years would be ideal but, for many, may not be realistic. This chapter discussed how the NYPD Police Pension is calculated under various scenarios. The calculation of the NYPD Police Pension is based on many factors: contribution rate, required amount, age at appointment, age at retirement, final average salary, years of service, value of annuity savings account, type of retirement, etc.

Before retiring, each NYPD member should take the time to fully understand the NYPD police pension, analyze his or her own situation, and project the value of the pension under different scenarios. After this analysis is done, the pre-retiree will be able to make a more informed and educated decision.

The appendix of this book has two case studies that readers may find informative. The first case study is a retirement projection for an NYPD member who has decided to continue working for the NYPD beyond twenty years. The second case study is a retirement income planning analysis for an NYPD member who has decided to retire from the NYPD after twenty years.

2

NYC DEFERRED
COMPENSATION PLAN

Introduction

The New York City Deferred Compensation Plan (NYC DCP) was established in 1986 and consisted of only the 457(b) plan. In the early years of the plan, many NYPD employees were hesitant to join because of the overall structure of the plan. A major disadvantage of the early plan was that the contributions made by employees were considered assets of NYC. This disadvantage was eventually corrected by having the employee contributions directed to a custodial account for the exclusive benefit of the employee. Some other disadvantages of the early plan were tax issues upon distribution and the lack of timely investment of employee contributions. Today, the overall structure of the plan has greatly improved, more investment choices are offered, and the NYC DCP has provided participants with educational materials. Currently, the NYC DCP offers a total of seven types of retirement plans: 457(b), Roth 457(b), 401(k), Roth 401(k), 401(a), NYCE IRA, and NYCE Roth IRA. Additionally, the distribution options available from the plans are very favorable to plan participants.

The NYC DCP has been a popular and simple way for many NYPD members to fund their retirement goals. This popularity and simplicity has resulted in the assets of the NYC DCP recently surpassing $10 billion.

Investment Funds

The seven retirement plans of the NYC DCP offer the same investment choices. Currently, seven core funds are offered:

- Stable Income Fund
- Bond Fund
- Equity Index Fund
- Socially Responsible Fund
- Mid-Cap Equity Fund
- International Equity Fund
- Small-Cap Equity Fund

In addition to the seven core funds, the NYC DCP also offers prearranged portfolios. The prearranged portfolios are useful for the participant who would rather select a time period of when distribution of the account will occur. For example, if a participant anticipates retiring and starting distributions from the NYC DCP account in the year 2020, the 2020 Fund may be appropriate.

In addition to the seven core funds and the prearranged portfolios, another investment choice is available in the NYC DCP. The self-directed option gives participants the ability to transfer up to 20% of their 457(b), 401(k), NYCE IRA, etc. balance to an outside brokerage account. Selecting the self-directed option allows the participant to select investments from thousands of different types of mutual funds: microcap, real estate, natural resources, international bonds, emerging markets, etc. Investing in individual stocks, individual bonds, exchange-traded funds, options, etc. is not permitted. Some NYPD members may find the self-directed option useful for the following reasons:

- Diversification. The current choice of funds in the NYC DCP may not provide true diversification for some participants. The financial markets consist of many different types of assets/investments not offered by the NYC DCP. As an example, all five of the NYC pension fund systems diversify across many different asset classes in order to reduce risk and attempt to maintain consistency of returns.
- This option allows the participant to add mutual funds of real estate, natural resources, microcap, international bond, emerging markets, dividend-paying companies, and many others.
- Some plan participants may consider their account to be "over weighted" in the US equity funds (small cap, mid cap, and equity index). Adding different asset classes may help to reduce the overall risk of the participants' account.

NYC DCP Fees

The fees charged to NYC DCP participants consist of three components: the quarterly administrative fee, the asset-based fee, and investment-management fees. The quarterly administrative fee is straightforward and is charged to a participant at a current rate of $20 per quarter for a total of $80 per year. The fee is clearly listed on a participant's account statement on a quarterly basis. The quarterly administrative fee is a significant part of the overall revenue stream of the NYC DCP and is used to pay for salaries, administrative support, recordkeeping costs, etc. The asset-based fee is based on the net asset values of each of the seven core investment options and the Treasury Inflation-Protected Securities (TIPS) fund used for the prearranged portfolios. Currently, the asset-based fee is .04%, or 4 basis points, and is also used for NYC DCP administrative expenses. This fee is not displayed on the participant's statements, but it is disclosed in the NYC DCP annual reports and other literature. Each of the core investment funds and the TIPS fund charge an investment-management fee, which reduces the overall return of each of the funds. This fee is used solely by the investment companies to operate each of the funds.

Comparing NYC DCP vs. a Retail IRA

When the NYC DCP first started, it was considered to be a cost-effective retirement-plan option for NYPD employees. Today, it is still somewhat cost effective, but because of the competiveness of the financial services industry and new financial products, a knowledgeable investor could have a personal retail IRA with extremely low ongoing expenses. The following is an example of a $200,000 NYC DCP 457(b) allocated as 30% bond fund, 25% equity fund, 15% mid-cap fund, 15% international fund, and 15% small-cap fund, compared to a retail IRA using low-cost index and exchange-traded funds.

NYC DCP 457(b) 2012 fees:
- $80 annual administrative fee

- $80 asset based fee
- $512 investment management fee
  Total fees = $672

Retail IRA fees:
- $0 annual administrative fee
- $0 asset based fee
- $240 investment-management fee
  Total fees = $240

NYC DCP Loans

An active NYPD member is eligible to take a loan from certain NYC DCP retirement plans. Only the NYC DCP 457(b) and the NYC DCP 401(k) have loan provisions; loans are not permitted from the Roth 457(b), Roth 401(k), 401(a), NYCE IRA, or NYCE Roth IRA. The following are a few highlights regarding NYC DCP loans:

- Retired NYPD members are not permitted to take a NYC DCP loan
- Minimum loan is $2,500
- Maximum loan is 50% of the account value in NYC DCP 457(b) or NYC DCP 401(k) *or* $50,000 reduced by any loan(s) from the NYC Police Pension Fund
- A maximum of two loans can be outstanding
- Interest rate on a loan is the prime rate (published in Wall Street Journal) plus 1%
- There is a $50 fee to process the loan and a quarterly maintenance fee of $8.75

NYC DCP Loan at Retirement

Retiring with an outstanding NYC DCP loan is similar to when an NYPD member retires with an outstanding pension loan. If the NYC DCP loan is not paid back, the retiree will be subject to income tax and possibly a 10% penalty on the total outstanding loan balance.

NYC DCP 457(b)

The NYC DCP 457(b) is the most prevalent plan for NYPD members. Generally, the main feature of the NYC DCP 457(b) plan is that distributions from the plan are not subject to the 10% early withdrawal penalty upon separation of service (in-service distributions are not permitted, except for hardship withdrawal or low-balance account). Contributions to the NYC DCP 457(b) plan are made by *active* NYPD employees using pre-tax dollars. Retired, vested, terminated, former employees, etc. are not permitted to contribute to the NYC DCP 457(b) plan. A significant advantage of the NYC DCP 457(b) plan is the separate treatment of contributions in reference to other retirement plans. This separate treatment gives the NYPD member an advantage over employees in the private sector. An NYPD employee could essentially contribute the maximum yearly contribution to both the NYC DCP 457(b) and the NYC DCP 401(k).

The money contributed to the NYC DCP 457(b) plan is not subject to federal, New York State, or New York City taxes, which reduces an employee's current gross income. The appreciation of the funds inside of the NYC DCP 457(b) plan are tax deferred; taxes are owed upon distribution to the participant or beneficiary.

NYC DCP 457(b) Contributions

Many NYPD members have been contributing to the NYC DCP 457(b) for years and have a substantial balance at retirement. The contribution rules are fairly straightforward, and the maximum amount that can be contributed each year may increase as a result of inflation. The NYC DCP participant selects a certain percentage of earnings, which are deposited into the participant's NYC DCP 457(b) account on a pre-tax basis. It is interesting to note that NYPD Police Pension Fund contributions (required & ITHP) are deducted first before the NYC DCP contributions are deducted from biweekly pay. The following is an example of how contributions to the NYC DCP 457(b) are calculated when a participant also contributes to the Police Pension Fund.

- Annual salary of $100,000
- Police Pension Fund contribution rate of 7.5%
- Election of ITHP waiver
- NYC DCP 457(b) plan contribution rate of 5%

Calculation:
- $100,000 × .075 = $7,500
- $7,500 contributed to the Police Pension Fund
- $100,000 – $7,500 = $92,500
- $92,500 × .05 = $4,625
- $4,625 contributed to the NYC DCP 457(b) plan
- Gross income reduced to $87,875

The NYC DCP 457(b) plan also allows some participants to use a three-year "catch up" (also referred to as the Deferral Acceleration for Retirement

[DAR]) contribution option. Some NYC DCP 457(b) participants may not be able to participate in the catch up because of their maximum contributions in each of the years they were eligible participants in the plan. For NYPD members considering the catch up, it may be beneficial to contact personnel at the NYC DCP regarding their eligibility. The following are some highlights of the three-year catch up provision:

- Should not be used in the year the participant intends to retire
- Can only be used once
- Up to twice the applicable annual contribution amount may be allowed
- Contributions are a fixed dollar amount per paycheck, not a percentage
- Funds are invested in the same way as the participant's regular contributions

NYC DCP 457(b) at Retirement

Years ago, the retiring NYPD member was required to select a distribution date for the funds inside of the NYC DCP 457(b). Today, the retiring NYPD member does not need to select any distribution date and has great flexibility in when and how distributions are received.

A decision that does have to be made at retirement is whether the retiree wants to leave the funds in the NYC DCP 457(b) or transfer the account to another type of retirement plan. For the retiree forty to fifty-nine years old, this decision should be easy. Leaving the funds in the NYC DCP 457(b) allows the retiree to take full advantage of the no 10% early distribution penalty feature. If the retiree were to transfer the NYC DCP 457(b) to a new retirement plan, the distribution rules of the new plan would apply. For example, assume a forty-five year old recent NYPD retiree decided to transfer his NYC DCP 457(b) to an IRA. Once the funds were transferred to the IRA, the retiree would be subject to the 10% early distribution penalty (unless an exception applies) if distributions were received before fifty-nine and one-half years old.

NYC DCP Roth 457(b)

The NYC DCP Roth 457(b) is similar to the regular NYC DCP 457(b), except the account is funded with after-tax dollars. The appreciation of the funds inside of the NYC DCP Roth 457(b) are tax-deferred, and distributions are tax-free, after certain conditions are met. In order to receive tax-free distributions from the NYC DCP Roth 457(b), the account must have been established for five years and at the time of distributions the participant is more than fifty-nine and one-half years old.

NYC DCP Roth 457(b) Contributions

Essentially, NYC DCP Roth 457(b) plan participants have chosen to pay taxes on their contributions now instead of in their retirement years. This choice may be worthwhile for NYPD members who have amassed significant assets in their pre-tax retirement accounts or for members who want to diversify their future tax obligations. The NYC DCP Roth 457(b) may also be an excellent choice for an NYPD member who is unable to contribute to a Roth IRA because of earnings greater than the threshold amount. No income-limit restrictions are applied when contributing to the NYC Roth DCP 457(b). For example, if an NYPD member has a salary of $125,000 and her spouse earns

$150,000, they would not be permitted to make an annual contribution to a Roth IRA. Although their combined income exceeds the income threshold for Roth IRA contributions, the NYPD member could contribute the maximum to the NYC DCP Roth 457(b) plan. In addition to contributing the maximum to the NYC DCP Roth 457(b) plan, the NYPD member could also contribute the maximum to the NYC DCP Roth 401(k) plan. For these two plans, contributions are considered separate and do not have to be aggregated.

The three-year catch-up provision (DAR) is available in the NYC DCP Roth 457(b) plan. Loans are not permitted from the NYC DCP Roth 457(b) plan.

NYC DCP Roth 457(b) at Retirement

Most retired NYPD members should consider transferring the NYC DCP Roth 457(b) to a Roth IRA in order to receive more favorable distribution features. A few retired NYPD members should not transfer to a Roth IRA because of age, the number of years the NYC DCP 457(b) has been established, and the overall purpose of the funds in the plan.

Qualified distributions from the NYC DCP Roth 457(b) can be entirely income tax free (Federal, state, & city) after certain conditions are met. There are three conditions for tax-free distributions:

1. Separate (retire) from the NYPD
2. At least fifty-nine and one-half years old
3. At least five taxable years since the initial contribution

Nonqualified distributions from the NYC DCP Roth 457(b) occur when the participant fails to meet one of the three conditions. The NYC DCP Roth 457(b) does not have the same distribution features of the Roth IRA. The NYC DCP Roth 457(b) does not allow for just the basis (tax-free portion) to be distributed first. The following is an example of a retired NYPD member who has received a nonqualified distribution (entire account balance) from the NYC DCP Roth 457(b).

Assumptions:
- Fifty-year old retired NYPD member
- Contributed a total of $50,000 to the NYC DCP Roth 457(b) while working for the NYPD
- Retired NYPD member's NYC DCP Roth 457(b) account has appreciated to $65,000
- Retired NYPD member receives a full distribution of the entire $65,000

Income tax implications:
- No 10% early withdrawal penalty even though the retiree is less than fifty-nine and one-half years old
- Income tax owed on only $15,000; the original $50,000 is considered a return of basis and is not subject to income tax

One of the disadvantages of the NYC DCP Roth 457(b) is that the original contributions cannot be solely distributed without income tax consequences. In the previous example, if the NYPD retiree only needed a distribution of $50,000; the $50,000 would be part taxable ($11,500) and part nontaxable ($38,500).

If a retired member, who is approaching seventy and one-half years old and still has a NYC DCP Roth 457(b), the account should be rolled over to a Roth IRA. The NYC DCP Roth 457(b) requires distributions at seventy and one-half years old, but the Roth IRA does not.

NYC DCP 401(k)

Two significant differences exist between the NYC DCP 457(b) and the NYC DCP 401(k): the 10% early distribution penalty and in-service distributions. The 10% early distribution penalty does apply to distributions from the NYC DCP 401(k) prior to the age of fifty-nine and one-half years old. A participant fifty-nine and one-half years old or older who has not retired from the NYPD could elect to receive distributions (in-service distribution) from the NYC DCP 401(k). Active NYPD members often fund the NYC DCP 401(k) after they have fully funded their annual NYC DCP 457(b) contribution.

NYC DCP 401(k) Contributions

NYC DCP 401(k) contributions are based on pre-tax earnings; account growth is tax-deferred; and distributions are taxable. As stated earlier, distributions prior to fifty-nine and one-half years old are subject to the 10% early withdrawal penalty. If an NYPD member can only afford to participate in one of the NYC DCP retirement plans, the NYC DCP 457(b) may be the better choice. Contributions to the NYC DCP 401(k) are treated as separate contributions from the NYC DCP 457(b). Therefore, an NYPD member could contribute the yearly maximum to both the NYC DCP 457(b) and the NYC DCP 401(k).

NYC DCP 401(k) at Retirement

At retirement, the retired NYPD member has a few choices regarding the NYC DCP 401(k).

- Leave the funds invested in the NYC DCP 401(k)
- Rollover to an IRA either at a bank, brokerage, or NYCE IRA
- Convert to a Roth IRA either at a bank, brokerage, or NYCE Roth IRA
- Take distributions, which are subject to taxes and penalty, if applicable

NYC DCP Roth 401(k)

The NYC DCP Roth 401(k) is funded with after-tax dollars. The appreciations of the funds inside of the NYC DCP Roth 401(k) plan are tax-deferred and distributions are tax-free after certain conditions are met. In order to receive tax-free distributions from the Roth 401(k), the account must have been established for five years and, at the time of distributions, the participant is more than fifty-nine and one-half years old.

NYC DCP Roth 401(k) Contributions

NYC DCP Roth 401(k) contributions are made with after-tax money; there are no income restrictions; and contributions are treated separately from the NYC DCP Roth 457(b). If an NYPD member is able to contribute to only one of the NYC DCP Roth accounts, the NYC DCP Roth 457(b) may be the better choice.

NYC DCP Roth 401(k) at Retirement

The distribution features of the NYC DCP Roth 401(k) are similar to the NYC DCP Roth 457(b). In most cases, the retired NYPD member should consider transferring the NYC DCP Roth 401(k) to a Roth IRA. At retirement, the retired NYPD member has a few choices regarding the NYC DCP Roth 401(k).

- Leave the funds invested in the NYC DCP Roth 401(k)
- Rollover to a Roth IRA at a bank, brokerage, or NYCE Roth IRA
- Take distributions, which are subject to taxes and penalty, if applicable

If a retired member is approaching seventy and one-half years old and still has a NYC DCP Roth 401(k), the account should be rolled over to a Roth IRA. The NYC DCP Roth 401(k) requires distributions at seventy and one-half years old, but the Roth IRA does not.

NYC DCP 401(a)

The NYC DCP 401(a), also known as the Savings Incentive Plan, is currently available only to active members of the LBA & CEA. The NYC DCP 401(a) is entirely funded by NYC, and participant contributions are not permitted. NYC will make a contribution (amount varies) to a participant's NYC DCP 401(a) if the participant contributes at least 1% of wages to the NYC DCP. Distributions from the NYC DCP 401(a) generally occur after separation of service and distributions prior to age fifty-nine and one-half are subject to the 10% early distribution penalty. A participant sixty-two years old or older who has not retired from the

NYPD could elect to receive distributions (in-service distribution) from the NYC DCP 401(a).

NYC DCP 401(a) at Retirement

At retirement, the retired NYPD member has a few choices regarding the NYC DCP 401(a).

- Leave the funds invested in the NYC DCP 401(a)
- Rollover to an IRA either at a bank, brokerage, or NYCE IRA
- Convert to a Roth IRA either at a bank, brokerage, or NYCE Roth IRA
- Take distributions, which are subject to taxes and penalty, if applicable

NYCE IRA

Most active NYPD members do not contribute to the NYCE IRA for various reasons: maximizing NYC DCP 457(b) contributions, maximizing pension contributions, exceeding income limits for deductibility, etc. The NYCE IRA may be suitable for a spouse of an NYPD member who desires his/her own retirement plan.

NYCE Roth IRA

The NYCE Roth IRA is funded with after-tax dollars. Many active NYPD members do not contribute to the NYCE Roth IRA for some of the same reasons as the NYCE IRA: funds are being directed to the NYC DCP 457(b), pension contributions, etc. The Roth IRA is an interesting retirement plan with some tremendous advantages; a later chapter will review it.

NYC DCP & Police Pension Fund Contributions

NYPD members often ask in what order based on affordability should contributions be made to either the NYC DCP or the Police Pension Fund? The following order of contributions may assist NYPD members (Tier II) in their decision making process:

1. Regular Police Pension Fund contributions (do not opt out of contributing)
2. ITHP Police Pension Fund contributions
3. Extra 50% Police Pension Fund contributions
4. NYC DCP 457(b) and/or NYC DCP Roth 457(b)
5. NYC DCP 401(k) and/or NYC DCP Roth 401(k)

Note: Members who are eligible to participate in the NYC DCP 401(a) may want to contribute at least 1% of earnings to the NYC DCP 457(b) or NYC DCP 401(k).

The advantage of contributing as much as possible to the Police Pension Fund before the NYC DCP is to take full advantage of the fixed rate of return (currently 8.25%) on members' Police Pension Fund ASF account. A larger ASF account at retirement affords the retiring NYPD member greater flexibility. The member could elect to leave the funds with the Police Pension Fund for an increased monthly benefit or elect to rollover the funds to a new retirement plan.

Chapter 2: Summary

This chapter reviewed the different retirement plans offered by the NYC Deferred Compensation Plan. In general, the NYC DCP is a suitable retirement plan while working, but depending on the type of retirement plan an individual participates in, the NYC DCP may not be the most advantageous in retirement.

The contribution and distribution rules of the various retirement plans can be overwhelming and confusing. Prior to receiving a distribution from any of the NYC DCP retirement plans, an individual should review any possible tax implications and penalties. Additionally, the participant should determine whether it would be advantageous to transfer the account to a different retirement plan in order to receive a more favorable distribution.

Readers of this book who have not retired from the NYPD should consider contributing to the NYC DCP Roth 457(b) instead of the NYC DCP 457(b). As reviewed in this chapter, the NYC DCP Roth 457(b) is funded with after-tax money and can provide federal and state tax-free distributions in retirement.

3

UNION ANNUITY PLAN

Five unions (PBA, DEA, SBA, LBA, & CEA) represent and assist NYPD members. The PBA, DEA, and SBA each have its own union annuity plan, whereas the LBA and CEA share the same plan. Years ago, it was nearly impossible for a participant to find out how the union annuity plan was invested. Today, all of the union annuity plans are more transparent, have a self-directed option, and mail account statements in a timely manner.

All of the union annuity plans are funded by NYC. The amount the city contributes is based on the union and its contract negotiations. Union members are not permitted to make ongoing contributions, although roll-overs into the plan may be permitted at retirement. Participant account balances are 100% vested, which means participants receive the value of the account if they quit or are fired from the NYPD.

Union Annuity Plan at Retirement

At retirement, the union annuity plan participant will have three choices available:

1. Distributions (total or partial)

Distributions from the union annuity plan are subject to federal tax and, in some cases, a 10% early withdrawal penalty. Distributions are not subject to NYS/NYC taxes but may or may not be subject to taxation by other states. Generally, the 10% early withdrawal penalty applies to the union annuity plan participant who receives a distribution and is less than fifty-nine and one-half years old. There is an exception to the 10% early withdrawal penalty if the union annuity plan participant retired from the NYPD at age fifty-five or older. The following is an example of a retired NYPD DEA member who has decided to receive a full distribution from the DEA annuity plan.

Assumptions:
*   Forty-five year old recently retired NYPD DEA member
*   Full distribution of $25,000 DEA annuity plan
*   NYS/NYC resident

Income tax implications:
*   Federal tax owed on full distribution amount of $25,000
*   20% federal tax withholding. The retiree receives a check in the amount of $20,000.
*   10% early withdrawal penalty; the retiree is less than fifty-nine and one-half years old. The 10% penalty is assessed when the retiree completes his federal tax return.
*   No NYS/NYC taxes

2. Rollover to another retirement plan

The union annuity plan can be rolled over to various types of retirement plans if the retiree wishes. Rolling over the union annuity plan may not be the wisest choice because of the possible loss of the tax-free NYS/NYC distribution feature. However, converting the union annuity plan to a Roth IRA may be an attractive alternative for some members. The features and advantages of the Roth IRA are reviewed in a subsequent chapter.

3. Leave funds with the annuity plan

Generally, if the funds in the union annuity plan are not currently needed, leaving the funds in the plan may make the most sense.

Rolling Over Funds into the Union Annuity Plan at Retirement

Some of the union annuity plans allow members to rollover certain funds into the plan at retirement. The funds that are commonly rolled over into the union annuity plan are the final distribution and the VSF DROP. The primary reason why retiring NYPD members elect to do this is to retain the NYS/NYC tax-free feature of the rolled over funds. Before performing the rollover, the retiring member should review the investment choices offered in the union annuity plan in order to determine if the choices are appropriate for the member's situation.

4

ROTH IRA

The Roth IRA is the ultimate wealth building retirement plan. Simply put, the Roth IRA is funded with after-tax money, grows tax-deferred, and distributions are tax-free after certain conditions are met. The conditions for receiving tax-free distributions are age fifty-nine and one-half or older (or disabled/death) and the Roth IRA is established for five years. Every NYPD member (active or retired) should establish and fund a Roth IRA in order to start the five-year time requirement. There are no required minimum distributions at age seventy and one-half, which makes the Roth IRA an attractive and cost-effective estate-planning mechanism. Three methods are available to fund a Roth IRA: annual contributions, rollovers, and conversions.

Annual Contributions

Making an annual contribution to a Roth IRA is permitted if the NYPD member has earnings that are either less than or within a specific range of the IRS phase-out range. The phase-out ranges for year 2013 are as follows:

- Filing status of single = $112,000 to $127,000
- Filing status of joint = $178,000 to $188,000
- Filing status of married filing separately = $0 to $10,000

For year 2013, an NYPD member who is less than fifty years old can contribute $5,500 per year to a Roth IRA. An NYPD member greater than fifty years old is eligible to contribute $6,500 per year to a Roth IRA. A Roth IRA contribution can be made during the period from January 1 of the current year until April 15 of the following year (for calendar year taxpayers). There are three methods available for NYPD members who are eligible to contribute to a Roth IRA.

- NYCE DCP Roth IRA
- Bank Roth IRA
- Brokerage Roth IRA

A taxpayer must have earnings to be able to contribute to a Roth IRA. In other words, if a retired NYPD member is only receiving pension income, an annual contribution to a Roth IRA would not be permitted.

Rollovers

At retirement, NYPD members who participated in either the NYC DCP Roth 457(b) or the NYC DCP Roth 401(k) have the option to rollover the funds into a Roth IRA. This may be an attractive feature for the retiree who desires more investment selection than what is offered by the NYC DCP. In addition, rolling over the NYC DCP Roth 457(b) or the NYC DCP Roth 401(k) to a Roth IRA may make sense for the older NYPD retiree. Both the NYC DCP Roth 457(b) and the NYC DCP Roth 401(k) require minimum distributions to be made at seventy and one-half years old, but with the Roth IRA, there are no minimum distribution requirements. A possible disadvantage of rolling over the NYC DCP Roth 457(b) into a Roth IRA is that the 10% early withdrawal penalty may apply from nonqualified distributions from the Roth IRA.

A retiring NYPD member could also rollover the final distribution into a Roth IRA. By electing this type of rollover, the retiring member would be subject to taxation in the current year. This option may be suitable for the retiree who would rather pay the taxes owed today than in the future. If the final distribution is a significant amount, the pre-retiree should calculate an estimate of the taxes owed before electing to rollover the funds to a Roth IRA.

Conversions

Conversion of a retirement plan to a Roth IRA is similar to a rollover to a Roth IRA except for most the conversion occurs at some point after retiring from the NYPD. The basic premise of a conversion is that the retiree decides to convert retirement plan assets (annuity fund, 457(b), 401(k), etc.) into a Roth IRA. In the past, conversions were only permitted if the taxpayer made less than $100,000. Tax laws changed in 2010, allowing anyone, regardless of income, to convert retirement plan assets to a Roth IRA. Although an annual contribution to a Roth IRA requires earnings (compensation), conversions do not. How do these conversions work? The best way to explain a conversion is to go through a simple example.

- Fifty year old married NYPD retiree
- Pension income of $80,000
- NYC DCP 401(k) balance of $75,000
- Fifty year old spouse W2 earnings of $35,000

If the NYPD retiree decides to convert the entire NYC DCP 401(k) balance ($75,000) at once into a Roth IRA, the couple's total income for the year would be $190,000. The $75,000 converted to a Roth IRA would be subject to ordinary income tax in the year of the conversion. Alternatively, the NYPD retiree could choose to convert only $10,000 of the $75,000 per year in order to possibly lessen the effect of income taxes. Ideally, funds (cash) should be available to pay the additional income taxes so the entire amount converted can go into the Roth IRA.

Wealth Building Power of the Roth IRA

In addition to the tax-free feature of distributions, many people are attracted to the Roth IRA because of its estate-planning attributes. The Roth IRA is a straightforward and cost-effective strategy for leaving money to the next generation. One of the significant advantages of a Roth IRA is that no required minimum distributions are required throughout the lifetime of the owner. In other words, the Roth IRA owner can decide to not take any money out of the Roth IRA and leave the entire account balance to a beneficiary(ies). The Roth IRA is the only retirement plan that has this feature; the 457(b), Roth 457(b), 401(k), Roth 401(k), and regular IRA all require minimum distributions at age seventy and one-half years. Using the same assumptions in the previous example, the table below displays the benefits of the Roth IRA when the spouse is the beneficiary.

Table #16				
Assumptions				
Roth IRA owner age: 50 years old				
Beginning balance of Roth IRA: $75,000				
Rate of return: 5%				
Roth IRA does not receive any distributions during lifetime				
Roth IRA owner age at death: 75 years old				
Beneficiary: Spouse 75 years old at time Roth IRA owner's death. The Roth IRA is rolled over and treated as "her own" Roth IRA				
Spouse's age at death: 85 years old				
Spouse receives $20,000 distribution per year beginning at age 75				
Age of Roth IRA owner	**Age of Spouse**	**Required minimum distribution**	**Distribution**	**Value of Roth IRA**
50	50	N/A	N/A	$75,000
51	51	N/A	N/A	$78,750
52	52	N/A	N/A	$82,688
53	53	N/A	N/A	$86,822
54	54	N/A	N/A	$91,163
55	55	N/A	N/A	$95,722
56	56	N/A	N/A	$100,507
57	57	N/A	N/A	$105,533
58	58	N/A	N/A	$110,809
59	59	N/A	N/A	$116,350
60	60	N/A	N/A	$122,167
61	61	N/A	N/A	$128,275
62	62	N/A	N/A	$134,689
63	63	N/A	N/A	$141,424
64	64	N/A	N/A	$148,495
65	65	N/A	N/A	$155,920
66	66	N/A	N/A	$163,716

67	67	N/A	N/A	$171,901
68	68	N/A	N/A	$180,496
69	69	N/A	N/A	$189,521
70	70	$0	$0	$198,997
71	71	$0	$0	$208,947
72	72	$0	$0	$219,395
73	73	$0	$0	$230,364
74	74	$0	$0	$241,882
75	75	$0	$20,000	$233,977
N/A	76	$0	$20,000	$225,676
N/A	77	$0	$20,000	$216,960
N/A	78	$0	$20,000	$207,808
N/A	79	$0	$20,000	$198,198
N/A	80	$0	$20,000	$188,108
N/A	81	$0	$20,000	$177,514
N/A	82	$0	$20,000	$166,389
N/A	83	$0	$20,000	$154,709
N/A	84	$0	$20,000	$142,444
N/A	85	$0	$20,000	$129,567

As shown in Table #16, the original Roth IRA owner started a $75,000 Roth IRA at age fifty and was able to grow the account to $241,882 by age seventy-four. No minimum distributions were required from age seventy until death at age seventy-five. The spouse received the Roth IRA at age seventy-five and decided to take a distribution of $20,000 per year. The spouse received $20,000 per year from age seventy-five until death at age eighty-five. The $20,000 per year (total distribution of $220,000) was received tax-free. At the spouse's death, there was still $129,567 in the Roth IRA available for a beneficiary(ies).

Let's see what happens if we continue the example to include a twenty-year-old beneficiary (grandchild). As per the rules of the Roth IRA, the beneficiary would be required to receive at least a minimum distribution from the Roth IRA. The required minimum distribution would also be tax free to the beneficiary.

Table #17		
Assumptions		
Beneficiary age when received: 20 years old		
Value of Roth IRA when received: $129,567		
Rate of return: 5%		
Required minimum distributions		
Age of Roth IRA beneficiary	**Required minimum distribution**	**Value of Roth IRA**
20	N/A	$129,567
21	$2,191	$133,854
22	$2,300	$138,247
23	$2,415	$142,744
24	$2,536	$147,345
25	$2,658	$152,054
26	$2,791	$156,865
27	$2,931	$161,778
28	$3,072	$166,795
29	$3,225	$171,909
30	$3,387	$177,118
31	$3,549	$182,425
32	$3,727	$187,820
33	$3,913	$193,298
34	$4,109	$198,854
35	$4,305	$204,492
36	$4,520	$210,196

37	$4,746	$215,959
38	$4,973	$221,785
39	$5,221	$227,653
40	$5,482	$233,553
41	$5,743	$239,487
42	$6,030	$245,431
43	$6,332	$251,371
44	$6,632	$257,308
45	$6,963	$263,210
46	$7,292	$269,079
47	$7,636	$274,897
48	$8,018	$280,624
49	$8,395	$286,260
50	$8,789	$291,784
51	$9,200	$297,173
52	$9,660	$302,371
53	$10,111	$307,379
54	$10,582	$312,166
55	$11,073	$316,701
56	$11,587	$320,949
57	$12,079	$324,918
58	$12,636	$328,528
59	$13,217	$331,738
60	$13,822	$334,502
61	$14,395	$336,833
62	$15,050	$338,625
63	$15,663	$339,892
64	$16,371	$340,516
65	$17,026	$340,516
66	$17,700	$339,842
67	$18,394	$338,440
68	$19,106	$336,257
69	$19,835	$333,234

70	$20,582	$329,314
71	$21,213	$324,566
72	$21,987	$318,808
73	$22,618	$312,130
74	$23,244	$304,493
75	$23,860	$295,858

As shown in Table #17, the twenty-year-old beneficiary received tax-free distributions from age twenty-one through seventy-five. The total tax-free distributions received by the beneficiary over the fifty-four year period were $544,891, with a remaining balance of $295,858 at the beneficiary's death. The beneficiary could have elected to receive the entire $129,567 tax-free at twenty years old, but that would have immediately ended the opportunity for ongoing distributions and appreciation of the Roth IRA.

This lengthy example demonstrated the wealth-building power and favorable tax treatment of the Roth IRA. The beginning balance of the original Roth IRA was only $75,000, but the total distributions were $764,891 ($220,000 to the spouse and $544,891 to the grandchild).

Chapter 4: Summary

This chapter reviewed the various methods to fund a Roth IRA: annual contribution, rollover, or conversion. Before converting retirement assets into a Roth IRA, the individual should carefully review the tax consequences. The wealth-building power and tax advantage of the Roth IRA was also reviewed and may be an attractive retirement plan for many NYPD members. The Roth IRA can be used to "tax diversify" retirement income or as an effective-estate planning mechanism. The basic concept of the Roth IRA is really quite simple: contribute after-tax money, the account grows tax-deferred, and all of the funds can be distributed tax free after certain conditions are met. If the NYPD member is not very familiar with the Roth IRA, numerous books and Internet sources are available.

5

SOCIAL SECURITY

The Social Security Act was signed into law on August 14, 1935, during the Presidency of Franklin D. Roosevelt. For the next two years (1935–1937) employers and employees were registered in order to implement the program. In 1939, the Social Security Act was amended to include benefits to spouses and minor children of a retired worker and also include survivor benefits. In January 1940, the first monthly retirement check was issued to a retired legal secretary, Ida May Fuller. Over a 35-year retirement period, Ms. Fuller collected a total benefit of $22,000. Automatic cost-of-living adjustments (COLAs) were implemented in 1975. The largest COLA increase between 1975 and 2012 was a 14.3% increase in 1980.

This chapter will provide a general overview of the Social Security retirement benefit; the Social Security disability benefit is not reviewed. The actual calculation of the Social Security retirement benefit will not be reviewed because of its complexity and its availability in other sources. What the future holds for Social Security is anyone's guess, so this chapter is based solely on current regulation.

Access Social Security Statement Online

Generally, the Social Security Administration no longer mails Social Security statements to most individuals. Individuals who are over the age of sixty and not receiving benefits will be mailed a Social Security statement. An individual's Social Security statement can be viewed online (once an account has been verified and established). Establishing an account and reviewing the statement annually will enable an individual to inform the Social Security Administration of any omissions and/or errors. Please note that the estimated monthly retirement benefits listed on the statement may not be entirely accurate for a retired NYPD member who only earns part-time income or no longer is employed. When preparing the estimate, the Social Security Administration makes an assumption using average earnings over an individual's working lifetime and assumes that the individual will continue to work and earn the prior year's wages.

Social Security Statement Retirement Benefit Basics

When an individual starts to plan for Social Security retirement benefits, a few important terms need to be understood:

- Full Retirement Age (FRA)
  -also referred to as Normal Retirement Age
  -individual receives the full retirement benefit from Social Security
  -FRA varies by what year an individual was born
  - Year of birth 1960 or later, FRA at sixty-seven years old

- Year of birth 1959, FRA at sixty-six years and ten-months old
- Year of birth 1958, FRA at sixty-six years and eight-months old
- Year of birth 1957, FRA at sixty-six years and six-months old
- Year of birth 1956, FRA at sixty-six years and four-months old
- Year of birth 1955, FRA at sixty-six years and two-months old
- Year of birth 1943-54, FRA at sixty-six years old
- Primary Insurance Amount (PIA)

  -PIA is received by individuals who start benefits at FRA
- Delayed retirement credits

  -individuals receive a larger retirement benefit if they delay payments until after FRA
- Reduced retirement benefits

  -individual receives retirement benefits before FRA

Receiving the Social Security Retirement Benefit Early

Most individuals elect to receive Social Security retirement benefits before full retirement age. Many begin at the earliest opportunity (62 years old) because they need the money to live, do not fully understand the benefits of delaying, or have convinced themselves that the Social Security system is going to collapse.

Depending on which year an individual was born, the reduction to the Social Security retirement benefit may be to 70–75% of the PIA when benefits are received at 62 years old. The following is an example of an individual with a full retirement age (FRA) of 66 and a PIA of $1,800.

- Benefits commence at sixty-two years old = $1,350

  -reduction of 25%

- Benefits commence at sixty-three years old = $1,440
  -reduction of 20%
- Benefits commence at sixty-four years old = $1,560
  -reduction of 13.33%
- Benefits commence at sixty-five years old = $1,680
  -reduction of 6.67%
- Benefits commence at sixty-six years old = $1,800
  -no reduction

Even though individuals who elect reduced retirement benefits receive COLAs, these adjustments have not been very significant recently.

Delaying the Social Security Retirement Benefit

For many retired NYPD members, it may make sense to receive distributions from a retirement plan and delay receiving Social Security retirement benefits beyond FRA. For every month the Social Security retirement benefit is delayed, the retiree receives a percentage increase until age 70. The following example is an individual with a full retirement age (FRA) of 66 and a PIA of $1,800.

- Benefits commence at sixty-six years old = $1,800
  -no benefit increase
- Benefits commence at sixty-six years and three-months old = $1,836
  -increase of 2%
- Benefits commence at sixty-seven years old = $1,944
  -increase of 8%

- Benefits commence at sixty-seven years and six-months old = $2,016
  -increase of 12%
- Benefits commence at sixty-eight years old = $2,088
  -increase of 16%
- Benefits commence at sixty-eight years and six-months old = $2,160
  -increase of 20%
- Benefits commence at sixty-nine years old = $2,232
  -increase of 24%
- Benefits commence at sixty-eight years and six-months old = $2,304
  -increase of 28%
- Benefits commence at seventy years old = $2,376
  -increase of 32%

For every year the retirement benefit was delayed, the individual received an 8% increase to the PIA. Delaying the retirement benefit until seventy years old resulted in a 32% higher monthly benefit.

Life Expectancy

Obviously, if we knew when we were going to die, all of us would know when to start receiving Social Security retirement benefits. Since our death date is unknown, it may be beneficial for an individual (single person) to plan to live to least eighty years old and delay the Social Security retirement benefit until 70 years old. Delaying a retirement benefit minimizes longevity risk. Simply put, the individual is trying to minimize the effects of living longer than expected.

Social Security Claiming Strategies

Single Person

Generally, the Social Security claiming strategies for a single individual are fairly straightforward and, for the most part, are based on the life expectancy of the individual. For example, if an individual (single person) expects to live only to eighty years old, claiming retirement benefits at age sixty-two would be optimal. Alternatively, if an individual expects to live well beyond eighty years old, claiming retirement benefits at age seventy would be ideal.

Married Couple

The Social Security claiming strategies for a married couple can be more complicated and varied. Recently, a few websites that review various Social Security claiming strategies have been created. Many of the websites require the user to enter personal information and pay a fee to view the recommended strategies. The following is a good example of a married couple using a simple claiming strategy.

Assumptions:
- John's age is sixty-six (has not elected his Social Security retirement benefit). John's FRA is sixty-six years old and his PIA is $2,200.
- Mary's age is sixty-two with a PIA of $1,800. Mary's FRA is sixty-six years old.

Strategy:
- Mary elects to receive a reduced benefit of $1,350 at sixty-two years
- John begins spousal benefits only at sixty-six years old and receives half of Mary's PIA benefit or $900.

- When John is seventy years old, he switches to his own Social Security retirement benefit. Because John delayed his own retirement benefit, it is now worth $2,904.
- The combined total is $4,254 ($2,904 + $1,350) when John is seventy years old and Mary is sixty-six years old.
- If John were to die at seventy-five years old, Mary would receive the higher benefit of $2,904

As this example shows, a couple should investigate different strategies before making any Social Security retirement elections.

Divorced, Widowed, Unmarried Minor Children and Disabled Children

In many instances, another individual may be able to claim a benefit related to another individual's Social Security. Believe it or not, a dependent grandchild could even receive a benefit based on a grandparent's earnings record.

In order for children to receive a benefit, the parent would need to be qualified for Social Security retirement benefits. The child (biological, adopted, or stepchild) would have to be unmarried and typically be less than eighteen years old (a disabled child has different rules). The following is an example of a child receiving a benefit based on the earnings record of a parent.

Assumptions:
- Mary's age is sixty-two, is a single parent and has a PIA of $1,500. Her FRA is sixty-six years old
- Mary's adopted daughter, Jane, is fourteen years old

Strategy:

- Mary elects to receive a reduced benefit of $1,125 at sixty-two years old
- Jane receives $750 (half of Mary's PIA)
- Mary and Jane would receive a combined total of $1,875 per month until Jane becomes eighteen years old. At that time, Mary would continue to receive her $1,125

Social Security retirement benefit rules regarding divorced individuals can be complicated. The following are a few highlights for a divorced individual using the ex-spouse's earnings record:

- When benefits can commence is based on whether the ex-spouse is living or deceased
- In most cases, the marriage lasted for ten years or longer
- Individual did not remarry. Doesn't matter if ex-spouse remarries.
- Individual is sixty-two years old or older
- Ex-spouse is entitled to Social Security retirement benefits

Divorced individuals should meet with Social Security personnel or a financial advisor who specializes in Social Security in order to determine retirement benefits that may apply for their particular situation.

Chapter 5: Summary

The purpose of this chapter was to provide the reader with a basic understanding of the Social Security retirement benefit. Many variables should
be reviewed before an individual decides when to begin Social Security
retirement benefits. For some, beginning benefits at age sixty-two makes
financial sense, but delaying the benefit may be advantageous for others.
Many more strategies other than the two provided in this chapter are available. For the most part, Social Security personnel are knowledgeable and
willing to help but may not be aware of all of the different claiming strategies. Meeting with a qualified financial advisor may be worthwhile before
deciding on a particular Social Security benefit.

6

TAXES

When an NYPD member gets ready to retire, understanding the various tax implications of retirement is critical. A mistake can be very costly and difficult, if not impossible, to correct. This chapter will review some of the common tax issues that retired NYPD members often encounter.

Tax Preparers

Before some of the tax issues are reviewed, a brief overview of the different types of tax preparers and the importance of selecting the right one is provided. This is one area where many NYPD members (retired and active) give themselves a lot of avoidable stress. Rule #1 is to locate a reputable, professional, and knowledgeable tax preparer. If you are still going to that tax preparer that works out of his basement and prepares tax returns with a pencil, it's time to move on. Yes, you will have to pay more, but doing so will be worth it in the long run. Of course, a good tax preparer needs to know general tax law, but the tax preparer should also be knowledgeable about the Police Pension Fund, NYC Deferred Compensation Plans, annuity funds, etc.

Tax Preparer Licenses/Certifications

During the past few years, IRS oversight has significantly increased over the tax preparation industry. The IRS has implemented a variety of requirements to protect the taxpaying public from unqualified and unethical tax preparers. Individuals paid to prepare tax returns will now have to take a competency exam. Additionally, tax preparers will have to register with the IRS and obtain a Tax Preparer Identification Number (PTIN). Believe it or not, before these new requirements, anyone could throw up a shingle and call his or her self a tax preparer.

Registered Tax Return Preparer (RTRP)
This type of tax preparer has satisfied the IRS requirements to prepare individual tax returns:

- Passed a one-time competency test
- Obtained a PTIN
- Passed a tax-compliance and suitability check
- Completes fifteen hours of continuing education per year

Enrolled Agent
An enrolled agent (EA) is a tax-practitioner license granted by the U.S. Department of Treasury. The IRS recognizes the enrolled agent as an elite status and is the highest credential the IRS awards. EAs specialize in areas of taxation and are authorized to represent taxpayers before all administrative

levels of the IRS in reference to audits, appeals, and collections. Enrolled agents, like attorneys and certified public accountants (CPAs), have unlimited practice rights. This means that they are unrestricted as to which taxpayers they can represent, what types of tax matters they can handle, and which IRS offices they can represent clients before. The following are the requirements to become and maintain EA status:

- Obtain a PTIN
- Pass a three-part comprehensive IRS test covering individual and business tax returns
- Pass a tax-compliance and suitability check
- Complete seventy-two hours of continuing education credits every three years

Certified Public Accountant
A CPA is a designation granted by the American Institute of Certified Public Accountants. CPAs receive their licenses from a state and have completed various education and experience requirements. CPAs work in many areas of business and may not specialize in taxation.

NYS Tax Advantages for NYPD Retirees

Retiring from the NYPD and remaining a NYS resident has some tax advantages. Currently, NYS has very favorable tax laws that benefit a retired NYPD member. The following income is not taxed by NYS:

- Pension from the NYPD
- VSF payment from the NYPD
- Annuity distribution from SOC, SBA, DEA, and PBA

- Social Security
- $20,000 pension/annuity exclusion if over fifty-nine and one-half years old

An NYPD retiree should carefully review the state and local taxes of an area they are considering retiring to. A handful of states do not have a state individual income tax, including Florida, Texas, Alaska, and New Hampshire, but most states tax all or a portion of an NYPD pension. In most cases, the nontaxable portion of the accidental disability pension is not taxed by states, but exceptions exist (New Jersey). The payment of state and local income taxes on retirement income should not be taken lightly. As the NYPD retiree ages, taxes paid become a significant disadvantage as the pension decreases in value as a result of inflation.

Pension Withholding (W4P)

In most cases, federal income taxes are withheld from NYPD pension payments. This is one area where many NYPD members have difficulty understanding and correctly implementing. Retirees often ask, "what tax rate will I pay on my pension?" This is not an easy question to answer because everyone's tax situation is different. For example, a single NYPD retired member who retires with a $50,000 pension and has no other earnings would be in a lower tax bracket than a married NYPD retired member who retires with a $50,000 pension and has a spouse who earns $100,000. When an NYPD member goes to the Police Pension Fund for a retirement counseling session, the member will need to decide how much federal tax withholding will be deducted from the monthly pension check. This is an important decision because the retiree does not want to be in a position at tax time in which not enough taxes were withheld. Retiring members may want to err on the side of caution and elect withholding that may be more than what they were withholding while working.

If not enough or too much is withheld, the retiree can easily correct this by mailing a new IRS form W4P to the Police Pension Fund.

Taxes and Retirement

Newspapers and financial magazines often report that retirees in general are more than likely to be in a lower income tax bracket during retirement. This may not be true for some NYPD retirees. Some NYPD retirees may be in higher tax brackets as a result of a combination of the pension benefit, Social Security retirement benefits, and distributions from retirement accounts. For these retirees, this becomes apparent very often when required minimum distributions (RMDs) take effect. Another often-overlooked item is that retirees do not normally have many deductions (mortgage interest, property taxes, unreimbursed employee expenses, dependent children, etc.), which may result in paying more income taxes in retirement.

NYC DCP 457(b) Tax Issues

As reviewed earlier, the NYC DCP 457(b) has a few favorable tax features, particularly the no 10% early withdrawal penalty regardless of age. Let's go through two examples of the tax implications of a distribution from the NYC DCP 457(b).

Example: 1

Assumptions:

• Fifty year old retired NYPD member

- Receives a one-time distribution of $30,000 from the NYC DCP 457(b)

Income tax implications:
- No 10% early withdrawal penalty even though the retiree is less than fifty-nine and one-half years old
- Retiree will receive $24,000 from the NYC DCP. The NYC DCP is required by law to withhold 20% from this type of distribution
- Retiree is subject to federal tax on the entire $30,000 distribution
- The $30,000 distribution is taxable by NYS and NYC, if applicable. There is no NYS pension/annuity exclusion for retirees less than fifty-nine and one-half years old.

Example: 2

Assumptions:
- Sixty-two year old retired NYPD member
- Receives a one-time distribution of $30,000 from the NYC DCP 457(b)
- Does not receive any other distribution(s) from his retirement plans

Income tax implications:
- Retiree will receive $24,000 from the NYC DCP. The NYC DCP is required by law to withhold 20% from this type of distribution
- Retiree is subject to federal tax on the $30,000 distribution
- $10,000 of the $30,000 distribution is taxable by NYS and NYC, if applicable. The retiree was able to take advantage of the NYS pension/annuity exclusion ($20,000) because he was over fifty-nine and one-half years old.

Occasionally, retired NYPD members decide to withdraw a significant amount of money from their NYC DCP 457(b) for the purpose of buying a second home, starting a business, etc. The retiree should calculate an estimate of what the tax implications (federal, state, and local) will be before requesting a distribution. Retirees who receive a large NYC DCP 457(b) distribution without calculating an estimate are unpleasantly surprised at tax time. The following is an example of a retiree who received a significant distribution from the NYC DCP 457(b).

Assumptions:
- Fifty year old retired NYPD member
- Receives a one-time distribution of $100,000 from the NYC DCP 457(b)
- Does not receive any other distribution(s) from his retirement plans

Income tax implications:
- Retiree will receive $80,000 from the NYC DCP. The NYC DCP is required by law to withhold 20% from this type of distribution
- Retiree is subject to federal tax on the entire $100,000 distribution
- The $100,000 distribution is taxable by NYS and NYC, if applicable. No NYS pension/annuity exclusion is available for retirees less than fifty-nine and one-half years old.

In this example, depending on the retiree's overall tax situation, the 20% federal tax withholding ($20,000) may not have been enough, and the retiree may owe even more at tax time. Additionally, the NYC DCP does not withhold NYS/NYC taxes on distributions; therefore, the retiree may also owe significant NYS and, if applicable, NYC taxes at tax time.

Exceptions to 10% Early Withdrawal Penalty

NYPD retirees need to avoid this IRS-imposed penalty whenever possible. Generally, the penalty is assessed when an individual receives a distribution from a retirement plan (does not apply to NYC DCP 457(b) distributions) and is less than fifty-nine and one-half years old. The penalty is an additional tax on the taxable amount of the money distributed. The penalty is added to the regular income taxes paid on the distribution. The following are some of the more common exceptions to the 10% early withdrawal penalty:

- Series of substantial equal periodic payments (72t)
- Distributions made to a beneficiary upon the death of the retirement plan owner
- Distributions due to retirement plan owner being totally and permanently disabled. Caution: the IRS does not use the same definition of disabled as the Police Pension Fund.
- Distributions from the Police Pension Fund and VSF DROP if retiree separated from service after fifty years old. The fifty year old exception does not apply if the retiree rolls over the final distribution and the VSF DROP into an IRA and takes a distribution from the rollover IRA.
- Distributions from the union annuity plan if retiree separated from NYPD service after fifty-five years old
- Distributions from an IRA to pay for college expenses for yourself, your spouse, your children, or grandchildren

Required Minimum Distributions

Generally, the IRS requires taxpayers to begin receiving distributions from most retirement plans by the age of seventy and one-half years. The overall purpose of required minimum distributions (RMDs) is to ensure that taxpayers do not just accumulate wealth in retirement accounts and leave the funds untaxed to a beneficiary(ies). Essentially, RMDs force taxpayers to remove some money from retirement accounts as taxable distributions. For some taxpayers, including retired NYPD members, RMDs can cause a significant change to a taxpayer's tax burden at both the federal and state level. For the most part, RMD rules are fairly simple to comply with, but in some instances can become complex. The following are some highlights of RMD rules:

- The federal government requires taxpayers to annually withdraw an amount from IRAs and/or employer-sponsored retirement plans even if the taxpayer does not "need" the money
- Distributions must be taken by April 1 of the calendar year following the year in which the taxpayer reaches the age of seventy and one-half
- A taxpayer can always withdraw more than the minimum amount, but if the taxpayer withdraws less than the required minimum amount, a significant federal penalty may apply
- RMD rules do not apply to Roth IRAs while the account owner is alive, but do apply to Roth 401k and Roth 457(b) plans
- Distributions are taxed at regular income tax rates
- Failure to comply with RMD rules may result in an IRS-imposed penalty of 50%

Let's go through an example of a retired NYPD member who has significant retirement assets and is subject to RMD rules.

Assumptions:

- Retired NYPD member with a birth date of April 1, 1942
- Rollover IRA (final distribution & VSF DROP) account balance of $425,000 as of December 31, 2011
- NYC DCP 457(b) account balance of $350,000 as of December 31, 2011
- Union annuity plan balance of $100,000 as of December 31, 2011
- Regular IRA account balance of $25,000 as of December 31, 2011

Calculation:

- Retired member will be 70 years old on April 1, 2012
- Retired member will be 70 ½ years old on October 1, 2012
- 2012 RMD must be distributed on or before April 1, 2013; this date is referred to as the required beginning date
- 2013 RMD must be distributed by December 31, 2013
- Minimum distribution factor used for 2012 is 27.4
- Rollover IRA 2012 RMD is $15,511
- NYC DCP 457(b) 2012 RMD is $12,774
- Union annuity plan 2012 RMD is $3,650
- Regular IRA 2012 RMD is $912
- Total 2012 RMD is $32,847

The total 2012 RMD of $32,847 is added to the NYPD retiree's income for the year. As reviewed earlier, the original owner of a Roth IRA is not subject to RMDs, making the Roth IRA a very attractive, tax-efficient retirement plan.

Taxation of SS Retirement Benefit

For the majority of NYPD retirees, 85% of the Social Security retirement benefits received will be federally taxable. The good news is that Social Security retirement benefits are not currently taxed by NY State.

Pension Contributions (414H) Tax Issues

Under current law, both the regular and the ITHP contributions to the Police Pension Fund are federally tax deferred but are taxed at the NYS/NYC level.

NYC 1127 Payments

Once retired, the NYPD member is no longer subject to the 1127 section of the NYC Charter. The NYC 1127 payments apply to certain active members who reside outside of NYC and are considered a condition of employment, not a tax.

Audits

Occasionally, active and retired NYPD members receive audit notices from the IRS and/or NY State. In many cases, the IRS audits are known as correspondence audits (CP2000), which means the matter can generally be resolved through the mail. Usually, a taxpayer receives a correspondence audit when the IRS computers do not match what was entered on the taxpayer's income tax return. If you receive a correspondence audit, please use the following as a guide:

- Do not ignore the notice

- Obtain the tax records for the year in question. If you do not have a copy of the tax return or are unable to obtain one from your tax preparer, request a Tax Return Transcript and a Tax Account Transcript (if applicable) from the IRS

- Do not ignore the due date on the letter received by the IRS. If you are not able to meet the deadline, request an extension. The difficulty in requesting an extension is trying to get to speak to an actual person at the IRS (you may be on hold for an extended period of time)

- Compare the letter received by the IRS with your tax return and determine what generated the audit

If you disagree with the IRS's findings, prepare a response and provide supporting documentation if needed

Chapter 6: Summary

This chapter reviewed the different types of certifications in the tax preparation industry and the importance of selecting a qualified and knowledgeable tax preparer. Many of the unique tax issues that apply to NYPD members were also reviewed. Understanding tax withholding on pension payments is a critical area of retirement planning that both pre and post retirees should understand. Nothing is worse than not withholding enough federal taxes from your NYPD pension and now owing money.

Unfortunately, for many NYPD retirees, taxes are a significant detriment to a comfortable retirement. By using some of the strategies presented in this book, specifically the Roth IRA, the NYPD retiree may be able to limit the damaging effects of taxes during retirement years.

7

ADVANCED TAX & RETIREMENT
PLANNING

This chapter will review more advanced tax and retirement planning strategies for the retiring NYPD member. Please note that the material presented may or may not be suitable for every retiring or retired NYPD member. These strategies may require the services of a knowledgeable tax professional to ensure compliance with various tax laws.

Series of Substantial Equal Periodic Payments

The series of substantial equal periodic payment (SSEPP) strategy, also commonly referred to as the 72(t) election [IRC §72(t)(2)(a4)(iv)], is an IRS provision that permits taxpayers to remove funds from a retirement plan and not be subject to the 10% early withdrawal penalty regardless of the taxpayer's age. As reviewed earlier, distributions from most retirement plans are subject to the 10% early withdrawal penalty if the taxpayer is less than fifty-nine and one-half years old. By electing the 72(t) election and complying with the rules, the taxpayer avoids the 10% early withdrawal penalty. Currently, there are three methods available when electing the 72(t) exception: minimum distribution, fixed amortization, and fixed annuitization. Under the rules of the 72(t) election, the taxpayer does not arbitrarily decide how much money to withdraw. Instead, the taxpayer needs to perform calculations in order to determine how much can be withdrawn under the three available methods.

Once the calculations are performed, the taxpayer would select one of the three available methods. Generally, once the method is selected, the taxpayer will be required to continue using the same method for a number of years.

Retired NYPD Member Using SSEPP-72(t) Example

The following is an example of a retired NYPD member using the 72(t) election in order to access funds prior to fifty-nine and one-half years old.

Assumptions:
- Fifty years old at retirement from NYPD
- Twenty-five years of service
- Distribution interest rate of 2.98%
- Life expectancy of 34.2 years
- Elected final distribution of $150,000 and rolled over to union annuity plan

- Rolled over VSF DROP funds of $60,000 to union annuity plan
- Union annuity plan balance of $40,000 prior to rollovers
- After completing the rollovers, the value of the union annuity plan is $250,000

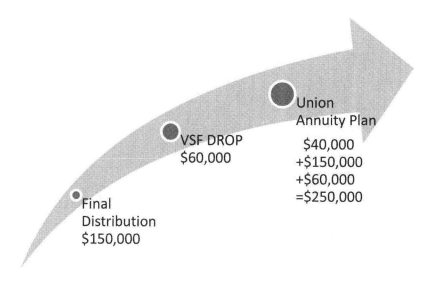

The retired NYPD member now has $250,000 available in the union annuity plan for the 72(t) election. Using the assumptions, the three methods can be calculated.

- Minimum distribution = $7,310 per year, or $609 per month
- Fixed amortization = $11,712 per year, or $976 per month
- Fixed annuitization = $11,757 per year, or $980 per month

Assume the NYPD retiree selects the fixed annuitization method and elects 72(t) at age fifty. Table #18 displays the results of the 72(t) election for the NYPD retiree.

Table #18				
Age	Beginning Balance	Distribution Year/month	Appreciation 4%	Ending Balance
50	$250,000	$11,757/$980	$9,530	$247,773
51	$247,773	$11,757/$980	$9,441	$245,456
52	$245,456	$11,757/$980	$9,348	$243,047
53	$243,047	$11,757/$980	$9,252	$240,542
54	$240,542	$11,757/$980	$9,151	$237,936
55	$237,936	$11,757/$980	$9,047	$235,227
56	$235,227	$11,757/$980	$8,939	$232,408
57	$232,408	$11,757/$980	$8,826	$229,477
58	$229,477	$11,757/$980	$8,709	$226,429
59	$226,429	$11,757/$980	$8,587	$223,259
60	$223,259	$11,757/$980	$8,460	**$219,962**

In this example, the NYPD retiree was required to distribute $11,757 per year, or $980 per month until fifty-nine and one-half years old. Once the retiree reaches fifty-nine and one-half years old, the 72(t) rules were complied with and the retiree can change or stop the distribution amount. As shown in the table, the retiree was able to distribute a total of $129,327 from age fifty to age sixty without incurring the 10% early withdrawal penalty.

An important 72(t) rule to remember is once the retiree elects to begin 72(t) distributions, the distributions must continue until age fifty-nine and one-half or for five years, whichever is later. If the retiree were to change the distribution amount prior to fifty-nine and one-half years old, the retiree would be subject to IRS-imposed interest and penalties. For example, if the retiree in the above example were to distribute $25,000 at age fifty-five, the interest and penalties would apply to the $25,000 and all of the distributions before age fifty-five.

The minimum distribution method works differently than the other two. Table #19, using the same assumptions as the previous example, displays the result if the retiree were to select the minimum distribution method.

Table #19				
Age	Beginning Balance	Distribution Year/month	Appreciation 4%	Ending Balance
50	$250,000	$7,310/$609	$9,708	$252,398
51	$252,398	$7,580/$632	$9,793	$254,611
52	$254,611	$7,883/$657	$9,869	$256,597
53	$256,597	$8,172/$681	$9,937	$258,362
54	$258,362	$8,471/$706	$9,996	$259,887
55	$259,887	$8,780/$732	$10,044	$261,152
56	$261,152	$9,099/$758	$10,082	$262,134
57	$262,134	$9,395/$783	$10,110	$262,848
58	$262,848	$9,735/$811	$10,125	$263,238
59	$263,238	$10,086/$841	$10,126	$263,278
60	$263,278	$10,448/$871	$10,113	$262,944

As shown in Table #19, the retiree was able to slightly increase yearly/ monthly distributions as he or she got older. The retiree received total distributions of $96,958 during the period and $262,944 remained at the completion of the 72(t) election.

72(t) Election and Final Distribution vs. No Final Distribution

In many ways, the 72(t) election creates an interesting added twist to the decision making process of whether to take the final distribution (final loan). Very often, NYPD pre-retirees do not select the final distribution because they have been incorrectly informed that the funds are not accessible until fifty-nine and one-half years old. The 72(t) election makes the final distribution funds available before fifty-nine and one-half years old without the 10% early withdrawal penalty as long as the rules are followed.

The following example shows how an NYPD retiree is able to take advantage of the 72(t) election to begin to make up a reduced pension as a result of selecting the final distribution.

Assumptions:
- Fifty years old at retirement from NYPD
- Twenty-five years of service
- Distribution interest rate of 2.98%
- Life expectancy of 34.2 years
- Final distribution available of $150,000
- VSF DROP funds of $60,000
- Union annuity plan balance of $40,000

Table #20 shows the decision the NYPD pre-retiree is trying to make.

Table #20		
	No Final Distribution	Final Distribution
Annual Pension	$90,603	$77,615
Monthly Pension	$7,550	$6,468
Difference of $1,082 per month		

If the NYPD pre-retiree elects the final distribution, the monthly pension is reduced by $1,082. Is there a tax efficient and penalty free method available for this pre-retiree to begin to make up the reduced pension? Yes, by using the 72(t) election.

In this example it works best if the retiree combines the $150,000 final distribution, the $60,000 VSF DROP, and the $40,000 union annuity plan. Once all of the rollovers are complete, the NYPD retiree would have $250,000 available for the 72(t) election. Next, the NYPD retiree would need to calculate the three 72(t) methods and select one of them. The following are the three calculated methods based on the previous assumptions:

- Minimum distribution = $7,310 per year, or $609 per month
- Fixed amortization = $11,712 per year, or $976 per month
- Fixed annuitization = $11,757 per year, or $980 per month

Assume the retiree selects the fixed annuitization method and elects distributions monthly. By selecting this method, the retiree was able to lessen the effects of the reduced pension, establish ownership of the final distribution, have the opportunity to earn interest/appreciation on the final distribution, and provide for a beneficiary in the event of an early death. Table #21 compares the pension with no final distribution and the pension with a final distribution and the 72(t) election.

Table #21		
	No Final Distribution	Final Distribution
Annual Pension	$90,603	$77,615
Monthly Pension	$7,550	$6,468
72(t) election	N/A	$980
Total monthly	$7,550	$7,448
Monthly difference of $102		

72(t) Election and a Significant Final Distribution Amount

The 72(t) election may be an effective retirement funding mechanism for the NYPD member who has a substantial final withdrawal amount and who retires in his or her early fifties. By electing the 72(t) election, the retiree is allowed to take the full final distribution and only be subject to the rules of the 72(t) election for a fairly short period of time. The following is an example of a fifty-four year old retiring NYPD member with a significant final distribution.

Assumptions:
- Fifty-four years old at retirement from NYPD
- Thirty years of service
- Distribution interest rate of 2.5%
- Life expectancy of 30.5 years

- Final distribution available of $415,000
- VSF DROP funds of $110,000
- Union annuity plan balance of $75,000

The retiree combines the $415,000 final distribution, the $110,000 VSF DROP, and the $75,000 union annuity plan into an IRA. Once all of the rollovers are complete, the NYPD retiree would have $600,000 available for the 72(t) election. Next, the NYPD retiree would need to calculate the three 72(t) methods and select one of them. The following are the three calculated methods based on the assumptions:

- Minimum distribution = $19,672 per year, or $1,639 per month
- Fixed amortization = $28,233 per year, or $2,353 per month
- Fixed annuitization = $28,350 per year, or $2,363 per month

The following table displays the result of the fifty-four year old retiree electing the fixed annuitization method at age fifty-five. As Table #22 indicates, the 72(t) election would only be in effect for a short period of time and after the age of sixty; the retiree would be permitted to change the dollar amount of the distribution or could even stop distributions if the retiree wished.

Table #22				
Age	Beginning Balance	Distribution Year/month	Appreciation 4%	Ending Balance
55	$600,000	$28,350/$2,363	$22,866	$594,516
56	$594,516	$28,350/$2,363	$22,647	$588,813
57	$588,813	$28,350/$2,363	$22,419	$582,882
58	$582,882	$28,350/$2,363	$22,181	$576,713
59	$576,713	$28,350/$2,363	$21,935	$570,298
60	$570,298	$28,350/$2,363	$21,678	$563,626

Final Word about the 72(t) Election

The 72(t) election is not for everyone. The retiree needs to fully understand how the provision works and determine if it is the best course of action to take. If the 72(t) election is not implemented correctly or is modified, the retiree will more than likely be subject to IRS imposed penalties and interest.

NYC DCP Retirement Plans at Participant's Death

As retired NYPD members age, they should begin to carefully review their various retirement plans. This is especially true for the retired member who may still have significant balances in the NYC DCP 457(b) and/or NYC DCP 401(k) plans. The retiree should perform some basic estate planning and educate the spouse/beneficiaries in order to avoid unfavorable consequences for the beneficiary(ies).

Spouse Sole Beneficiary of NYC DCP 457(b) Example

Assumptions:
- Retired NYPD member dies at age seventy-five
- Did not establish a NYCE IRA for spouse
- NYC DCP 457(b) balance of $300,000 at death
- Seventy-five year old spouse (not employed by NYC and did not retire from NYC employment) of deceased NYPD member is the sole beneficiary

Result:
- The beneficiary spouse has a few choices regarding the NYC DCP 457(b) balance of $300,000

1. Leave money with the NYC DCP and establish an Inherited Distribution Account

2. Rollover to a new IRA or existing IRA

3. Disclaim within nine months of retired NYPD member's death

If the surviving spouse were to select choice #1, the following would occur:

- The surviving spouse would not be able to select any beneficiaries

- Any money not withdrawn from the Inherited Distribution Account would pass to the surviving spouse's estate (normally, this should be avoided) upon the surviving spouse's death

A simple way to correct this would have been for the retired NYPD member to establish a spousal NYCE IRA (if the retired member was satisfied with the NYC DCP) before his death. Establishing a spousal NYCE IRA would have allowed the spouse beneficiary to simply transfer the NYC DCP 457(b) assets into her own NYCE IRA. In this example, result #2 may be more appropriate because the rollover IRA would allow the surviving spouse to elect a beneficiary(ies) and the IRA would be treated as her own.

Two Adult Non-Spouse Beneficiaries of NYC DCP 457(b) Example

Assumptions:

- Retired NYPD member dies at age seventy-five

- NYC DCP 457(b) balance of $300,000 at death

- Fifty year old son and forty-eight year old daughter of deceased NYPD member are the beneficiaries

Result:

- The non-spouse beneficiaries have a few choices regarding the NYC DCP 457(b) balance of $300,000
  1. Leave money with the NYC DCP and establish an Inherited Distribution Account
  2. Rollover to an Inherited IRA
  3. Disclaim within nine months of retired NYPD member's death

An advantage of the NYC DCP Inherited Distribution Account and the Inherited IRA is that distributions received by the beneficiary(ies) are not subject to the 10% early distribution penalty. A disadvantage of both the NYC DCP Inherited Distribution Account and the Inherited IRA is that the beneficiary(ies) is not permitted to elect a beneficiary. Another disadvantage is that the beneficiary(ies) must begin distributions no later than December 31 of the calendar year immediately following the calendar year in which the participant died.

Inherited IRA Basics

The following are some bullet points regarding Inherited IRAs for non-spouse beneficiaries.

- Inherited IRAs cannot be commingled with other types of IRA assets
- Distributions from non-spouse inherited IRAs are not subject to the 10% penalty
- There is no sixty-day rollover rule for inherited IRAs. If you withdraw the money, it's taxed
- If the original IRA owner was required to take a distribution in the year of death and didn't, then the beneficiary must take it.

- Stretch the inherited IRA, if possible and try to extend the distribution of the account as long as possible

This area of retirement planning often causes a lot of confusion for the retiree or beneficiary(ies). If a retired NYPD member has significant balances in any retirement plan, it may be worthwhile to review the circumstances with a qualified financial professional. Additionally, there are many rules regarding when distributions must occur and if not followed correctly, may result in IRS-imposed penalties.

Additional Advanced Retirement Planning Topics

The following are some additional advanced retirement planning topics (beyond the scope of this book) which require a thorough review of an individual's tax, financial situation, and overall goals.

- Tax planning for the accidental disability NYPD retiree
- Conversions of retirement accounts to a Roth IRA in reference to accidental disability NYPD retirees
- Conversions of multiple retirement accounts to a Roth IRA
- Large sum distributions from various retirement accounts
- Strategies regarding required minimum distributions (RMDs)
- Correcting omitted or inaccurate RMDs
- Distribution planning for beneficiary(ies) of retirement accounts
- 72(t) election from separate retirement plans
- NY State tax planning in reference to distributions from a rollover IRA funded by a final distribution or VSF DROP
- Distribution analysis of NYC DCP Roth 401(k) and Roth 457(b) vs. the Roth IRA

Chapter 7: Summary

This chapter reviewed a few advanced retirement planning topics that may not be suitable for everyone. The election of the 72(t) is a useful retirement income strategy but should only be used after a complete understanding of the various rules and methods. The 72(t) election is somewhat restrictive because once it is elected; the individual is not able to modify (in most cases) the payment plan without incurring significant IRS-imposed penalties and interest.

Every retired NYPD member should review their various retirement plans (NYC DCP 457(b), IRA, Roth IRA, etc.) in order to determine if retirement assets will pass to a beneficiary(ies) in a tax-efficient and simple manner.

8

WHO TO TURN TO FOR ADVICE

Active NYPD members and retirees are often bombarded with financial information from many sources. These sources may include the Internet, newspapers, magazines, unions, seminars, the "expert" at work, etc. This information or "advice" may be overwhelming, inaccurate, or confusing at times. Sometimes it appears that everyone has a "theory" or opinion on how to retire or how to invest money. If an active NYPD member or retiree decides to seek help from a financial planner, financial advisor, tax preparer, insurance salesperson etc., a few basic guidelines are provided below:

- Always remember that this is your hard-earned money
- Ask questions
- Thoroughly understand any financial product(s) you are considering purchasing

- Do not be pressured into buying any financial product without a complete understanding of the fees, commissions, restrictions, tax implications, etc.
- Nothing is free

Ten Basic Questions to Ask a Financial Planner/Advisor

1. What experience do you have?
2. What are your qualifications/credentials?
3. What services do you offer?
4. What is your approach to financial planning?

   -type of clients

   -viewpoint on investing
5. Will you be the only person working with me?
6. How will I pay for your services?
7. How much do you typically charge?
8. Could anyone besides me benefit from your recommendations?
9. Have you ever been publicly disciplined for any unlawful or unethical actions in your professional career?
10. Can I have it in writing?

    -a written agreement that details the services to be provided

Five Specific Questions to Ask a Financial Planner/ Advisor

1. Do you know what Series of Substantial Equal Periodic Payments (72t election) means?
2. Do you know which type of retirement plans the final distribution can be rolled into?

3. What are the federal and NY State tax consequences of not rolling over the taxable portion of the final distribution?

4. At retirement, should I rollover my NYC DCP 457(b) account to an IRA?

5. At retirement, should I rollover my union-sponsored annuity plan to an IRA?

Credentials

The "alphabet soup" of the various credentials in the financial planning/advice area is mind boggling. For some consumers, it may be very difficult to sort through all of them and make a decision. Of course, having a credential should not be the sole reason in choosing an individual to help with your finances, but it is usually a good place to start your search. The following credentials are the better known ones:

Certified Financial Planner®

At a minimum, a CFP® has successfully completed the following coursework:

- General principles of financial planning
- Insurance planning
- Employee benefits planning
- Investment planning
- Income tax planning
- Retirement planning
- Estate planning

A CFP® professional has also met the following requirements:

- Examination. A ten-hour, two-day comprehensive exam covering over one-hundred financial-planning topics.
- Experience. A minimum of three years of financial-planning-related work experience.
- Ethics. A code of ethics and other requirements are to be followed.
- Education. A bachelor's degree (or higher) and at least thirty hours of continuing education every two years.

Enrolled Agent

An EA is a tax-practitioner license granted by the U.S. Department of Treasury. The IRS refers to the enrolled agent as an elite status and is the highest credential the IRS awards. EAs' specialize in areas of taxation and are authorized to represent taxpayers before all administrative levels of the IRS in reference to audits, appeals, and collections. Only EAs, CPAs, and attorneys may represent taxpayers before the IRS. The EA license is granted after the successful completion of exams or in some instances after five years of relevant work experience at the IRS.

Chartered Financial Consultant

The chartered financial consultant (ChFC) is a financial planning designation granted by the American College in Pennsylvania. The following are the requirements of a ChFC:

- Completed a comprehensive curriculum in financial planning.
- Passed a series of written examinations.

- Has met specific experience requirements.
- Maintains ethical standards.

Chartered Life Underwriter

The chartered life underwriter (CLU) is an insurance and financial-planning designation granted by the American College in Pennsylvania. The requirements of the CLU are similar to the ChFC, but the CLU may be more familiar with insurance products.

Chartered Financial Analyst

A chartered financial analyst (CFA) is a professional designation granted by the CFA Institute. Of all the various credentials, the CFA may be the most rigorous to achieve. In order to become a CFA, an individual would need to pass three levels of exams covering accounting, economics, ethics, money management, and security analysis. Additionally, there is a three-year work experience requirement and a bachelor's degree requirement.

Certified Public Accountant

The certified public accountant (CPA) is a designation granted by the American Institute of Certified Public Accountants. CPAs have completed various education and experience requirements. CPAs work in many areas of business and may not specialize in taxation and/or retirement planning.

The CPA/PFS is a certified public accountant with a personal financial specialist (PFS) designation. This designation is granted to CPAs who have completed a level of financial planning work experience, passed a personal financial planning exam, and completed continuing education requirements.

Methods of Compensation

The different forms or methods of compensation paid to financial planners or advisors may also be confusing to the consumer. Prior to meeting with a prospective advisor, individuals should research and understand these different methods of compensation. The following are some common forms of compensation paid to financial advisors.

Fee Only

A fee-only advisor is compensated solely by the client and does not accept commissions from selling insurance or investment products. The fee-only advisor may charge a set fee based on a specific project or charge a fee based on the amount of time spent working with a client.

Fee or Asset Based

The fee- or asset-based advisor is often confused with the fee-only advisor. An asset-based advisor charges a fee based on the amount of the assets under management. For example, a fee-based advisor may charge a yearly fee of 1.5% of the total value of a client's portfolio. For a $100,000 portfolio this yearly fee would be $1,500.

Commissions

An advisor who charges a commission is compensated based on the financial product that is sold to the client.

Fee Based and Commissions

An advisor may charge a combination of fees and commissions. The fees charged may be for the amount of work done to develop financial planning recommendations and commissions are received from any products sold.

APPENDIX

CASE STUDIES

Case Study #1

Case study #1 will review a retirement-planning scenario based on a fictional couple, John and Mary Smith. The case study is presented to the reader to highlight the benefits of compounding interest, ongoing contributions to retirement plans, and delaying retirement from the NYPD.

Background

John Smith
- Forty-five years old
- NYPD Sergeant
- Appointment date July 1993
- Twenty years of service
- $130,000 gross salary

- Contributes 7.15% of gross pay to the Police Pension Fund
- Contributes to the NYC Deferred Compensation 457(b) plan

Mary Smith
- Forty-five years old
- Registered nurse
- Employed at a hospital
- $75,000 gross salary
- Contributes to a 403(b)
- Plans to retire at age fifty-five

John and Mary Smith were married in 1993, have two children (ages fourteen and twelve), and own a home on Long Island. When the Smiths were first married, they did not have a lot of money saved. They were fortunate enough to be able to buy a home with help from Mary's grandmother. John is trying to decide if he should retire from the NYPD but doesn't think he has any professional skills that would be marketable outside of the NYPD. John still enjoys his job, but like any job, it can be stressful at times. As John and Mary's children get closer to college age, John is concerned about the uncertainty of a new job. He is considering working for the NYPD until age fifty-five so he can fully retire at the same time as his wife. Mary intends to continue with her nursing profession and has increased her hours since the children have gotten older. John and Mary have been able to consistently contribute to their retirement accounts due to both of them working and by living within their means. They have become accustomed to contributing to their retirement accounts and are confident that they will be able to continue to do so. John and Mary intend to provide some financial assistance to their children in order for them to attend a public college in New York State. The Smiths anticipate that their mortgage will be paid off by the time they are 57 years old. Once retired, they plan to do extensive traveling and volunteer work.

John's current assets

Police Pension fund account balance: $175,000

NYC 457(b) balance: $200,000

Union annuity: $30,000

Mary's current assets

403(b) plan from hospital $55,000

Roth IRA $8,000

John & Mary jointly owned current assets

Stock brokerage account $10,000

Market value of home $425,000

Children's college money (from grandparents)

529 Plan #1 $15,000

529 Plan #2 $12,000

John Smith retirement projections

John has made estimated pension calculations and retirement projections based on 20 and 30 years of service to help decide if he should retire from the NYPD or not.

Retirement assumptions based on twenty years of service:

- Retire at age forty-five from the NYPD
- NYC Deferred Compensation 457(b) Plan balance of $200,000

- Union annuity balance of $30,000
- VSF annual benefit of $12,000 once retired
- Yearly pension benefit of $55,800 (pre-tax) after taking final distribution
- Pension final distribution (final loan) amount of $162,500

Calculations:
- Twenty years of service
- FAS $130,000
- Required amount $125,000
- Pension fund balance $175,000
- Overage (excess) $50,000
- 50% of FAS $65,000
- Value of overage $4,089
- Final distribution "cost" ($13,289)
- Yearly pension benefit pre-tax $55,800
- Monthly pension benefit pre-tax $4,650

Retirement assumptions based on thirty years of service:
- Retire at age fifty-five from the NYPD
- NYC Deferred Compensation 457(b) Plan balance of $450,000 (5% rate of return and contributions of $10,000 per year)
- Union annuity balance of $67,000
- VSF DROP of $120,000
- Yearly pension benefit of $93,080 (before taxes) after taking final distribution
- Pension final distribution (final loan) amount of $520,500

Calculations:

- Thirty years of service
- Final average salary (FAS) $150,000
- Estimated value of 1/60 $23,300
- Required amount $125,000
- Pension fund balance $533,000
- Overage (excess) $408,000
- 50% of FAS $75,000
- Value of overage $38,254
- Estimated ITHP actuarial benefit $6,500
- Final distribution "cost" ($49,974)
- Yearly pension benefit pre-tax $93,080
- Monthly pension benefit pre-tax $7,757

Table #23 below compares the twenty-year retirement vs. the thirty-year retirement.

Table #23		
	20 year retirement	**30 year retirement**
Annual NYPD pension benefit	$55,800	$93,080
NYPD pension fund balance	$175,000	$533,000
NYPD pension final withdrawal	$162,500	$520,500
Annual VSF benefit	$12,000	N/A
VSF DROP	N/A	$120,000
NYC DCP 457(b)	$200,000	$450,000
Union annuity	$30,000	$67,000

As the above table indicates, John will be able to significantly increase his overall wealth and receive a pension that is 67% more at a thirty-year retirement than a twenty-year retirement. At retirement, John, fifty-five years old, will have a few different options available to fund his retirement.

1. Rollover his final distribution ($520,500), VSF DROP ($120,000), and union annuity ($67,000) for a total of $707,500 into a rollover IRA and elect 72(t) for a five-year period.

2. Receive distributions from his $450,000 NYC DCP 457(b) plan without the 10% early distribution penalty. Distributions will be subject to federal taxes and possibly NY State taxes.

3. Live off his $93,080 annual NYPD pension benefit and the $12,000 annual VSF payment and allow his retirement accounts to appreciate.

If John decides to stay on the NYPD until fifty-five years old, he may want to consider contributing to the NYC DCP Roth 457(b) instead of the NYC DCP 457(b). Contributing to the NYC DCP Roth 457(b) will reduce some of his future tax liabilities.

Case Study #2

Case study #2 will review a retirement income planning scenario based on a fictional single person, Susan O'Reilly. The case study is presented to the reader to highlight a retired NYPD member who has decided to fully retire at age fifty after completing twenty years of service.

Background

Susan O'Reilly

- Fifty years old
- Third Grade Detective
- Appointment date July 1993
- Twenty-years of service
- $125,000 gross salary
- Contributes 6.3% of gross pay to the Police Pension Fund
- Contributes to the NYC Deferred Compensation 457(b) plan
- Assumes a life expectancy to ninety years old

Susan O'Reilly Retirement Projections

Susan has decided to retire after twenty years of NYPD service and wants to fully retire and remain a NY State resident. She plans to fund her retirement using the following retirement assets:

1. NYPD defined benefit pension
2. VSF annual benefit of $12,000 once retired
3. Yearly distributions from the NYC Deferred Compensation 457(b) plan from ages fifty to sixty

4. Distributions from rollover IRA for ages sixty to ninety
5. Begin Social Security retirement benefits at age seventy

Retirement assumptions based on twenty years of service:
-   Retire at age fifty from the NYPD
-   NYC Deferred Compensation 457(b) Plan balance of $150,000
-   Union annuity balance of $20,000
-   Yearly pension benefit of $53,151 (pre-tax) after taking final distribution
-   Pension final distribution (final loan) amount of $123,000

Calculations:
-   Twenty years of service
-   Final average salary (FAS) $125,000
-   Required amount $120,000
-   Pension fund balance $135,000
-   Overage (excess) $15,000
-   50% of FAS $62,500
-   Value of overage $1,299
-   Final distribution "cost" ($10,648)
-   Yearly pension benefit pre-tax $53,151
-   Monthly pension benefit pre-tax $4,429

For ages fifty through sixty years, Susan plans to receive distributions from her NYC DCP 457(b) plan since there is no 10% early withdrawal penalty. Susan will pay federal tax on the NYC DCP distributions but will not have to pay NYS/NYC taxes because of her mortgage interest, real estate taxes, etc. The final distribution ($123,000) and the union annuity ($20,000) will be rolled over to an IRA and she assumes a 5% appreciation rate for ten years. Susan will have the following retirement funds to use from age fifty to sixty:

1. $4,429 monthly NYPD pension benefit
2. $1,500 monthly distribution from the NYC DCP 457(b) plan
3. $12,000 annual VSF payment
   Total annual gross income pre-tax: $83,151
   Total monthly gross income pre-tax: $6,929

For ages sixty through ninety, Susan plans to receive distributions from her rollover IRA, which has appreciated to $232,932 and the 10% early withdrawal penalty no longer applies because she is over fifty-nine and one-half years old. Susan will pay federal tax on the rollover IRA distributions, but will not have to pay NYS/NYC taxes because she will take advantage of the $20,000 NY State pension/annuity exclusion. The NYC DCP 457(b) plan no longer has a balance since she used it from age fifty to sixty. Susan will have the following retirement funds to use from age sixty to seventy:

1. $4,429 monthly NYPD pension benefit
2. $1,275 monthly distribution from the rollover IRA
3. $12,000 annual VSF payment
   Total annual gross income pre-tax: $80,451
   Total monthly gross income pre-tax: $6,704

Although Susan's gross monthly income was decreased by $225 per month, her mortgage will have been fully paid off at age sixty.

For ages seventy through ninety years old Susan plans to continue to receive distributions from her rollover IRA and also receive her Social Security retirement benefit. By delaying her Social Security retirement benefit, Susan was able to take full advantage of the delayed retirement credit. Susan will pay federal tax on the rollover IRA distributions, but will not have to pay NYS/NYC taxes because she will continue to take advantage of the $20,000 NY state pension/annuity exclusion. The Social Security retirement benefit will be 85% taxable by the federal government, but will not be taxed by NY State. Susan will have the following retirement funds to use from age seventy to ninety:

1. $4,429 monthly NYPD pension benefit
2. $1,275 monthly distribution from the rollover IRA
3. $2,200 monthly Social Security retirement benefit
4. $12,000 annual VSF payment
   Total annual gross income pre-tax: $94,850
   Total monthly gross income pre-tax: $7,904

Susan's retirement planning is straightforward, but she was able to take advantage of the no 10% early withdrawal penalty of the NYC DCP 457(b) and at the same time avoid NY state taxes on the NYC DCP 457(b) distributions. She also was able to invest her final withdrawal and union annuity in a rollover IRA for a ten year period in order to achieve account appreciation. Additionally, Susan was able to take advantage of the Social Security delayed retirement credit provision in order for her to maximize her Social Security retirement benefit.

ABOUT THE AUTHOR

Peter Thomann, EA, CFP® is the president of Thomann Tax & Asset Management, Inc. (TTAM), and is a retired member of the New York City Police Department. Now an Enrolled Agent and Certified Financial Planner® with years of experience helping clients with tax preparation, tax planning, retirement planning, and investment advice, Thomann holds a master's degree in financial planning and a bachelor's degree in accounting. Thomann has counseled hundreds of active and retired members of the NYPD on retirement planning, and has been a featured speaker at NYPD retirement planning seminars and training sessions. To learn more about the services of TTAM and to stay up to date with the latest tax and retirement planning news specific to active and retired NYPD members, visit www. thomanntax.com.

Made in the USA
Lexington, KY
03 May 2013